I saw this and thought of you. You're to only person I know who has read LesMis. thought you might appreciate it!

Happy Birthday,

Jane

52
LITTLE LESSONS
From
Les Misérables

52

LITTLE LESSONS

From

Les Misérables

BOB WELCH

NELSON
BOOKS

An Imprint of Thomas Nelson

Published in Nashville, Tennessee, by Nelson Books, an imprint of Thomas Nelson. Nelson Books and Thomas Nelson are registered trademarks of HarperCollins Christian Publishing, Inc.

Published in association with the literary agency of WordServe Literary Group, Ltd., www.wordserveliterary.com

Thomas Nelson titles may be purchased in bulk for educational, business, fund-raising, or sales promotional use. For information, please e-mail SpecialMarkets@ThomasNelson.com.

Unless otherwise indicated, Scripture quotations are taken from the Holy Bible, New International Version®, NIV®. Copyright © 1973, 1978, 1984, 2011 by Biblica, Inc.™ Used by permission of Zondervan. All rights reserved worldwide. www.zondervan.com

Scripture quotations marked ESV are taken from THE ENGLISH STANDARD VERSION. © 2001 by Crossway Bibles, a division of Good News Publishers.

Scripture quotations marked KJV are from the King James Version (public domain).

Library of Congress Cataloging-in-Publication Data

Welch, Bob, 1954-
  52 little lessons from Les Misérables / by Bob Welch.
    pages cm
  ISBN 978-1-4002-0666-7 (hardback)
1. Hugo, Victor, 1802-1885. Misérables. 2. Faith in literature. 3. Christianity in literature. I. Title. II. Title: Fifty-two little lessons from Les Misérables.
PQ2286.W45 2014
843'.7--dc23

2014005366

Printed in the United States of America

14 15 16 17 18 RRD 6 5 4 3 2 1

Les Misérables *(Lay-mee-zay-rahbl)*—
The Miserable Ones, or "The Poor"

Contents

CONTENTS

Contents

Contents

LIST OF CHARACTERS

PRIMARY CHARACTERS

Jean Valjean (Zhan Val-zhan)—ex-convict who begins
life anew while being tracked down by a tireless police
inspector

Bishop Myriel—compassionate bishop whose mercy
on Valjean changes the ex-convict's life (full name:
Monseigneur Charles François-Bienvenu Myriel)

Inspector Javert (Jah-ver)—letter-of-the-law police
inspector whose obsession is to bring justice to Valjean

Cosette (Ko-zet)—Fantine's daughter, saved by Valjean
from the clutches of a cruel and cunning innkeeper
couple, the Thénardiers

Fantine (Fahn-teen)—unmarried, working-class girl
whittled to her core by poverty; mother of Cosette

Marius Pontmercy (Mar-ee-us Pohn-mair-see)—idealistic
student who falls in love with Cosette

The Thénardiers (Ten-are-dee-ays)—husband and wife

innkeepers bent on exploiting all who come near, including Cosette

OTHERS

Bamatabois (Bam-ah-tah-bwah)—prospective "customer" whose degradation of Fantine triggers her wrath

Champmathieu (Chomp-mot-two)—poor, uneducated man who is identified, tried, and almost convicted as being Jean Valjean

Enjolras (Ahn-jol-rahs)—leader of the student revolutionary group Friends of the ABC (ah bay say), so-named from a play on the French word *abaissés* (the "lowly" or "abased")

Éponine (Epp-oh-neen)—daughter of the Thénardiers who secretly loves Marius and redeems herself with that love

Fauchelevent (Fosh-luh-vohn)—man saved by Valjean in Montreuil-sur-Mer who later helps Valjean in a Paris convent

Gavroche (Gav-rosh)—likable street urchin—and son of the Thénardiers—who gives his all to the student revolutionary cause

Gillenormand (He-lare-nor-ma)—Marius's grandfather, a devout monarchist and self-seeking part of Paris's bourgeois class

Madeleine (Mad-eh-lenn)—name Valjean assumes when he comes to Montreuil-sur-Mer

Petit Gervais—twelve-year-old boy from whom Valjean steals a coin

Colonel Georges Pontmercy (Zhorzh Pohn-mair-see)—

Marius's father, a courageous officer of Napoléon's who
grudgingly allows Marius's grandfather to bring up his son
Félix Tholomyès (Thol-o-mee-es)—college student in Paris
who abandons Fantine after getting her pregnant

PLACES

Digne (Din-yay)—town in French Alps where Valjean
meets the bishop
Montfermeil (Moan-fer-may)—town where the
Thénardiers and Cosette live
Montreuil-sur-Mer (Mon-twee-soor-Mair)—town where
Valjean assumes the name "Madeleine" and begins anew
Petit-Picpus (Pet-teet-Pic-poo)—convent in Paris where
Valjean and Cosette live
Toulon (Too-lohn)—prison on coast of southern France
where Valjean spends nineteen years

Author's Note

THE FIRST QUESTION YOU ASK YOURSELF WHEN BEGINNING the challenge of conveying the life lessons of *Les Misérables* is: *Really?* You couldn't have chosen a less complex story, one not based on a book whose unabridged Signet paperback edition stretches to 1,463 pages?

"*Les Misérables* etches Hugo's view of the world so deeply in the mind that it is impossible to be the same person after reading it," writes Graham Robb in *Victor Hugo: A Biography*. "[And] not just because it takes a noticeable percentage of one's life to read it."[1]

The second question—assuming you've considered the first and, as I do, believe the richness of the story outweighs the task of plowing through a brick-thick book—is: On what will you base such lessons?

Should you base them on Victor Hugo's 1862 work, considered by many to be the greatest social novel of all time? On the musical, the world's longest running, and seen by more than sixty-five million people in forty-two countries? Or on the more than thirty movie versions, the latest of which, in 2012, garnered eight Academy Award nominations and won a Golden Globe award for best picture?

If, over a century and a half, *Les Misérables* has evolved into something of an artistic trinity, it would seem appropriate to respect it as such. Although Hugo's original story will be the foundation on which I build, each of the three incarnations is unique and worthy on its own. Taken as a whole, they provide a grand expression of how Hugo himself describes his story: "a progress from evil to good, from injustice to justice, from falsehood to truth, from night to day, from appetite to conscience, from corruption to life; from bestiality to duty, from hell to heaven, from nothingness to God."[2]

To read Hugo's words is to see the brushstrokes of an artist creating a literary masterpiece; to watch the musical, first done in 1980 in Paris, is not only to hear and see *Les Miz* but to *feel* it as if you're sitting in an emotional wind tunnel; and, finally, to watch the 2012 movie is not only to surprise yourself at having loved an entire *sung-through* movie but also to marvel at the fascinating blend of nineteenth-century France and twenty-first-century moviemaking technology.

As these three streams tumble down through time, the inspirational lake they create can speak to us all. Hugo writes:

I don't know whether it will be read by everyone, but it is meant for everyone . . . Social problems go beyond frontiers. Humankind's wounds, those huge sores that litter the world, do not stop at the blue and red lines drawn on maps. Wherever men go in ignorance or despair, wherever women sell themselves for bread, wherever children lack a book to learn from or a warm hearth, *Les Misérables* knocks at the door and says: "open up, I am here for you."[3]

I analyze Hugo's work not as a *Les Misérables* expert but as a fellow life traveler smitten with the story and as a firm believer that one of the gifts of great literature, theater, and movies is self-discovery. The question shouldn't be only, what did the story say about France back then? But also, what can it say to me where I am right now?

I came to love *Les Miz* late, not as a decades-long fan or drama critic, but as a journalist and author fascinated by the twining of life and faith, having written, among sixteen other books, *52 Little Lessons from It's a Wonderful Life.*

My scope of seeing theatrical presentations of *Les Misérables* ranges from a world-tour show spearheaded by original producer Cameron Mackintosh in Vancouver, British Columbia's three-thousand-seat Queen Elizabeth Theatre to a dinner-theater presentation by Actors Cabaret in Eugene, Oregon, so intimate that, en route to a preshow potty break, I ran into a few Toulon prisoners and a French soldier in the hallway. Soon I found myself watching 1935, 1952, and 1999 movie versions of *Les Misérables.* I watched and rewatched the 2012 movie, the songs replaying in my mind as if I were a bus, and Valjean, Javert, and the rest of the cast were riders who refused to get off.

Though Hugo was religiously eclectic and, like us all, morally flawed, his book is undeniably spiritually seasoned with death and resurrection, law and grace, wrongdoing and redemption. In short, it is seasoned with God stuff, the contemplation of which Hugo himself applauds in the book, offering a gentle rebuke to those who display "the haughty air of superiority and compassion assumed toward the philosophy that sees God . . . It makes one think of a mole exclaiming, 'How I pity them with their sun.'"[4]

So powerful is *Les Misérables* that actors in the musical have found themselves changed by being part of it. Israeli singer David Fisher, who played Valjean, said, "I know that God was standing over (Alain) Boublil and (Claude-Michel) Schönberg when they wrote the piece. There's no doubt in my mind about that."[5]

Geronio Rauch, an Argentine Catholic who played Valjean, talked of how Hugo's character begins the story almost as if he's an animal. "And then he starts a journey, a Christian journey, the same journey as Jesus but without the same fateful death. I find myself crossing myself on the stage and, when I do, I'm praying inside. I'm saying, 'Father, Son, Holy Spirit.'"[6]

When Hugo's book reached America in 1862, Boston's *Atlantic Monthly* was critical of it, in part because it found *Les Misérables* "abstractly Christian."[7] If it is now universally loved by the public, might some of that affection relate to that very reason—to the story's God-shaped, grace-based undertones?

The life lessons that follow, then, are spiritually inclined because *Les Misérables* is undoubtedly spiritually inclined, a story richly leavened with sustenance for the soul. Regardless of the vast differences we bring to the table as readers of books and searchers for meaning, we're bound by a common need to be nourished by the things that matter.

And that, above all, is what *Les Misérables* is all about.

CONTEXT MATTERS

The loftiest things are often the least understood.[1]
—*LES MISÉRABLES*

OUR FAMILY WAS VACATIONING IN THE SHADOWS OF OREGON'S Cascade Mountains when I noticed my college-age niece buried in a book. Not any book. *Les Misérables.* Not any version. A French edition.

Some of you, like her, know *Les Misérables* inside and out. You know Marius's full name is Baron Marius Pontmercy. You could offer a play-by-play on the Battle of Waterloo; Hugo spends no fewer than forty-nine pages on it. You could enliven the dullest dinner party with an array of *Les Miz* trivia, say, that Colm Wilkinson, who plays the bishop of Digne in the 2012 movie, originated the role of Jean Valjean in the London and New York stage productions.

For others, the story is new. So, to begin, let us beg the pardon of the French-reading nieces of the world and offer a fast-forward version of the story. Why do so? Because *context matters.* Building the scaffolding of a story helps us understand the nooks and crannies within. Knowing a little prepares us to know more. And knowing more helps us discover deeper truths.

So we begin: It is October 1812 in the south of France. Jean Valjean, a former tree pruner with uncommon physical strength, is released from prison after serving nineteen years—five for stealing a loaf of bread to feed his sister's family, and another fourteen for frequent attempts to escape. Turned away, scorned, and beaten by others—his "yellow card" passport marks him as trouble—Valjean is taken in by a kindhearted bishop.

Valjean is amazed at the bishop's kindness. And yet he later slips into the night having stolen the man's silverware. But when Valjean is caught by police and returned, the bishop insists that the silverware was a gift to Valjean—and claims he had forgotten the candlesticks, which were meant for him too. The doubting police agree to release Valjean.

The bishop bids him farewell. "Do not forget, ever," he tells the forgiven man, "that you have promised to use this silver to become an honest man."[2]

After a misstep, Valjean does so, even though it means changing his identity. In Montreuil-sur-Mer, as "Monseiur Madeleine," he revolutionizes a bead factory that brings fabulous wealth to him and economic sustenance to the village. He is appointed mayor.

In Paris, a young woman, Fantine, is abandoned by the wealthy student she loved and who fathered her child. Knowing she won't be able to find work in her hometown of Montreuil-sur-Mer if her indiscretion is found out, she arranges for innkeepers, the Thénardiers, to look after little Cosette in the neighboring town of Montfermeil. She then goes to work in Madeleine's factory, sending the Thénardiers money for the care of her child.

But she loses her job when it is learned she has a child out of wedlock.

When Madeleine lifts a cart to save the life of a man pinned beneath it, his strength awakens suspicion in a witness to the incident. Chief of police Javert remembers seeing such strength in only one man: the prisoner Jean Valjean when Javert was serving as a guard in Toulon.

The Thénardiers demand more money to care for Cosette. To support her daughter, Fantine grudgingly sells her hair, her teeth, and, ultimately, her body as a prostitute. When Javert arrests her and insists she be sent to jail, Madeleine intervenes and releases her.

Fantine falls ill and longs to see Cosette. Madeleine vows to make these arrangements. Meanwhile, though, Javert learns of another criminal who has confessed to being Jean Valjean. When Javert tells Madeleine this information, the real Valjean is presented with a convenient "out." Instead, after considerable inner turmoil, he confesses his true identity to spare the man. When Javert arrives at Fantine's bedside to arrest Madeleine, the young woman dies—but not before Valjean promises her he will take care of Cosette.

Valjean is sent to prison by Javert for breaking parole. Later, he escapes and buys Cosette from the Thénardiers, swindlers who have neglected and physically abused the girl. Realizing Javert is on his trail, Valjean finds refuge for himself and Cosette in a Paris convent, where he works as a gardener.

Years pass. As Valjean and his adopted daughter walk through the streets of Paris, a young law student, Marius Pontmercy, takes notice of Cosette—and she of him. Valjean grows fearful of losing her. Marius and Cosette meet when Valjean visits the apparently needy neighbors of Marius, who turn out to be the Thénardiers. In an extortion scam, they plan to have Valjean robbed by cohorts. Marius alerts Javert, the local police inspector, to foil the plot, and Valjean escapes before Javert can identify him.

Meanwhile, Marius joins a band of student radicals who fuel a political uprising against the French royalist government. When the Thénardiers' daughter, Éponine, helps Marius meet Cosette, Valjean feels further threatened. He plans to take Cosette to England to keep her away from Marius. Heartbroken at the news, Marius reconciles that he will die in the inevitable student clash with government troops.

When a barricade is built and violence breaks out, the students capture Javert as a spy. Éponine, who secretly loves Marius, saves his life by throwing herself in front of a bullet. While dying, she hands him a letter from Cosette. The grieving Marius sends a reply to her through Gavroche, a street urchin.

Valjean intercepts the note, realizes the depth of Cosette's love for Marius, and heads for the barricade to join the student revolutionaries' cause. When Javert is apprehended as a spy, Valjean offers to execute him. But once alone with Javert, he sets his pursuer free. Marius is wounded. As the French army storms the barricade, Valjean escapes into the sewer system with the unconscious Marius, bumping into Thénardier along the way.

Javert outwits Valjean and arrests him as he emerges from the sewer with Marius. Valjean pleads to allow the wounded young man to be taken to his grandfather. Javert allows it, but he feels so conflicted about Valjean's mercy and his failure to bring the man to justice that he commits suicide.

Marius recovers. He reconciles with his grandfather with whom he's had a falling-out and, with the man's blessing, marries

Cosette. Instead of informing Cosette and Marius that he was responsible for saving the young man's life, Valjean reveals his criminal past. Marius wants nothing more to do with the man. The shattered Valjean prepares to die. But Marius accidentally learns from Thénardier that it is Valjean who saved his life. Marius tells Cosette. The two come to Valjean's side, and, reconciled with Cosette, Valjean dies in peace.

Whew.

If that seems rushed, it should. It's the distillation of 1,463 pages of Hugo's novel into fewer than one thousand words, the literary equivalent of trying to scoop the Pacific Ocean into a thimble. So what follows is a broader—and more leisurely—voyage across this sea of significance.

FAME BRAGS; LOVE WHISPERS

Love one another. He declared that to be complete. He desired nothing more.[1]

—HUGO, ON THE BISHOP'S PRIORITIES

ALTHOUGH THE MOVIE VERSION OF *LES MISÉRABLES* BEGINS with the cultural chasm between Jean Valjean and Javert, Hugo opens his book with a fifty-eight-page exploration of Monseigneur Charles Francois-Bienvenu Myriel, the bishop of Digne. The man whose grace toward Jean Valjean leaves the former convict inalterably changed, which, in turn, changes so many whom Valjean touches.

Who is this man whom the author finds so important? Myriel, we learn, had been born into a regal family. His father was a superior court judge, and Myriel is expected to follow in his father's footsteps. Myriel is "elegant, graceful and witty," writes Hugo, "passionate" and "violent."[2]

"His early years had been devoted to worldly pleasures." As was the custom among privileged families, he marries a young woman handpicked by his father. He appears to be headed for the spotlight. In the pre-TV and YouTube days of late-1700s Paris, that might not have meant a particularly bright spotlight, but Myriel's trajectory clearly points him toward fame and fortune. "Charles Myriel," writes Hugo, "had attracted a great deal of attention."[3]

Then, in 1789, comes the French Revolution—the real deal, not the 1832 street riots portrayed in *Les Misérables*—and everything changes. Political and social upheaval topple the country's absolute monarchy—a form of government in which the monarch exercises ultimate governing authority as head of state and head of government. Myriel flees to Italy. His wife dies after an extended illness. When he returns to France, he is a changed man.

Why the turnaround? Hugo is agonizingly silent on the subject, one of the quirks of an author who thinks nothing of chattering on for dozens of pages about battles and sewers and convents but ignores a question that begs to be answered. All we know is that Myriel emerges from Italy as a priest, is later appointed a bishop, and settles into a life of obscurity in a small village in the Alps.

If it is a life thin on notoriety, it is thick with meaning. The bishop, Myriel, is "an upright man."[4] He insists that the twenty-six indigent patients in the cramped hospital in Digne take over his palace while he moves to their narrow, two-story building. His personal budget is one-sixth what he gives to the poor. His kindness earns him the nickname "Bienvenu," which means "Welcome." His lone luxuries are his silverware and candlesticks.

Myriel visits neighboring villages not aboard a gold-trimmed carriage with an entourage but alone on a donkey. Rich or poor, Myriel relates to people well, exuding "the very eloquence of

Christ," writes Hugo. "He could say the loftiest things in the simplest languages; and as he could speak all dialects, his words penetrated every soul." He defends those who cannot defend themselves, especially women and the poor. "The faults of women, children, and servants," we read, ". . . are the faults of their husbands, fathers, and masters, of the strong, the rich, and the wise."[5]

When the local curé—or parish priest—refuses to spend time with a man condemned to die for the murder of another, Myriel walks beside the convict. Talks to him. Prays with him. "The sufferer, so desolate and overwhelmed the day before, was now radiant with hope," we are told. "He felt that his soul was reconciled, and he trusted in God."[6]

Among other priests, Myriel is a loner. "Monseigneur Bienvenu, a humble, poor, private person, was not counted among the rich miters," writes Hugo. "This was plain from the complete absence of young priests around him. We have seen that in Paris he did not fit in. No glorious future dreamed of alighting upon this solitary old man."[7] Myriel, meanwhile, likes serving other people.

So, would Myriel's life "cut it" in modern-day America? Would it conform to what we hold near and dear? Not so much. We like advancement. We like fame and fortune. We ascribe greatness to those who can get onstage and sing or dance for millions—or win some reality TV show. Or those who make a tackle on a football field and flex their muscles to milk the crowd for praise—as if what they've really done, instead of flattening a ball carrier, is find a cure for cancer. We like "Likes" on our Facebook pages and thousands to follow us on Twitter.

But Myriel—who in earlier years "had attracted a great deal of attention"—is the living embodiment of 1 Thessalonians 4:11: "Make it your ambition to lead a quiet life." Not in frittering away opportunity so he won't be bothered. But in involving himself in the lives of others.

In so doing, he reminds us that dignity—the stuff that really matters—is not loud and proud and onstage. Instead, it whispers in the obscure places and touches the obscure people. And, in quiet ways, it changes the world.

Knock and the door
will be opened

Have you knocked at that one there?[1]
—A woman in Digne who takes pity on Valjean

In Digne as a recently released convict, Jean Valjean is turned away for this job and turned away from that inn. He is even turned away when he asks a jailer if he can stay for a night; the irony is that Valjean, though technically a free man, is a slave to his past—so much so that he is willing to go to jail as a means of survival. In Hugo's no-room-in-the-jail scene, Valjean resembles the prodigal son, who became so desperate to survive that "he longed to fill his stomach with the pods that the pigs were eating." Alas, "no one gave him anything" (Luke 15:16).

"Everybody has driven me away," Valjean tells a woman who takes enough pity on him to help.

"Have you knocked at every door?" she asks.

"Yes," he says.

"Have you knocked at that one there?"

"No."

"Knock there."[2]

Because of that door—the bishop's door—what he finds isn't just a hot meal, a glass of wine, and a warm bed.

What he finds is life. Grace. God.

Better yet, God finds him. And not with the suspicion of Inspector Javert. Not with the unreachable you-must-be-this-tall-to-enjoy-the-ride standards, but with the open arms of a father of grace welcoming home the prodigal son.

In a material world, where we're honored for what we look like and what we own and how high we score on the SAT, God looks deeper. "The LORD does not look at the things people look at," says 1 Samuel 16:7. "People look at the outward appearance, but the LORD looks at the heart."

Like Javert, we can look completely put together. Fully in control. Totally committed to a noble cause. "Our addictions make us cling to what the world proclaims as the keys to self-fulfillment: accumulation of wealth and power, attainment of status and admiration; lavish consumption of food and drink, and sexual gratification without distinguishing between lust and love," writes Henri J. M. Nouwen. "These addictions create expectations that cannot but fail to satisfy our deepest needs . . . I am the prodigal son every time I search for unconditional love where it cannot be found."[3]

So we stumble in the dark, clinging to blind pride to prove ourselves right. Until, desperate, we knock. Then, as Matthew 7:7–8 says, everything changes. "Ask and it will be given to you; seek and you will find; knock and the door will be opened to you. For everyone who asks receives; the one who seeks finds; and to the one who knocks, the door will be opened."

Lesson 4

Every personal encounter matters

I am in this world to care not for my life, but for souls.[1]
—Monseigneur Myriel, the bishop of Digne

Les Misérables pivots on a single act of kindness shown by Monseigneur Myriel. It changes the life of Jean Valjean. Above all, it reminds us that a single act of kindness can last a lifetime—and beyond.

When the just-released-from-prison Valjean shows up at the bishop's door one night, the two men have little in common. At age forty-four, Valjean has been a slave to injustice, cruelty, and coldhearted men. Prison has left him nearly as much animal as man. He is branded as a convict—literally (No. 24,601[2]) and figuratively—and his newfound freedom promises little hope.

At age seventy-five, Myriel voluntarily chooses to eschew privilege to serve others less fortunate. Thus, when he welcomes Valjean into his home and offers him food, wine, warmth, and a bed, it is nothing extraordinary for him. In his eyes, the extraordinary thing in this situation is the stranger.

The bishop welcomes Valjean unconditionally. "Come in," he says, not even waiting to see who is at the door, a sign of unconditional acceptance. He not only listens to Valjean divulge his life as an ex-con but, when he finishes, turns to his servant and says, "Madame Magloire, another place please."[3]

When Valjean himself warns that his papers point out he is "highly dangerous"—he'd never have cut it as a door-to-door salesman—and asks if there is a stable where he might sleep, the bishop again turns to his servant. "Madame Magloire," he says, "put some sheets on the bed in the alcove."[4]

The bishop looks at this man and sees not his past but his future, not an ex-prisoner but promise. He looks at this encounter not as a threat or an inconvenience but as an honor. "Madame Magloire, set the places as near the fire as you can," he instructs. Then, turning to Valjean, he says, "You must be cold, monsieur."[5]

Madame Magloire, on the other hand, sees Valjean with suspicion at best. Earlier, at the market, she had heard of an "evil-looking runaway . . . lurking somewhere in town."[6] It's no accident she has not placed the silverware and candlesticks on the table.

But the bishop believes Valjean is redeemable. After the freed man expresses wonder that the bishop would welcome a former convict into his house, Myriel says, "This is not my house; it is Christ's . . . You are suffering; you are hungry and thirsty; you are welcome." And later, in a paraphrasing of Luke 15:7, says, "There will be more joy in heaven over the tears of a repentant sinner than over the white robes of a hundred just men."[7]

That said, the ultimate test of the man's concern for this stranger comes in the morning, after the police catch Valjean leaving the village with the bishop's silverware. Why hadn't Valjean taken the candlesticks too? he asks in front of the police. After all, says Myriel, they had been given to him as gifts along with the silverware and dishes.

The police are dumbfounded, Jean Valjean even more so. In a life of darkness, he has never experienced such light. And this single act of kindness will, in time, change him forever. Will, in essence, turn him into an honest man. Will, indirectly, save Cosette, Marius, and many others.

Why? Because one man—Monseigneur Charles Francois-Bienvenu Myriel—refuses to look at another man with the scorn that others had, that his own servant had.

His example begs a question that too many of us—myself included—hesitate to ask ourselves: Would I do the same?

I think of too many encounters when, with subtle self-righteousness, I've assumed the worst of others. When I've played the part of the servant, and instead of considering a stranger's needs, I've considered my candlesticks and silverware—the operative word being *my*. When I've thought of an encounter as an inconvenience instead of an honor. When I've smugly considered that this is *my* house, not Christ's. When I've ignored the wisdom of Hebrews 13:2 that the bishop understood so well: "Do not forget to show hospitality to strangers, for by so doing some people have shown hospitality to angels without knowing it."

Lesson
5

Even the coldest
heart can thaw

*Then his heart swelled, and he burst into tears. It was
the first time he had wept in nineteen years.[1]*

—Hugo, on Valjean

When the police officers return after catching the
former convict with the bishop's silverware, all Myriel has to do
is say nothing—what's easier than that?—and Valjean will be
hauled back to prison.

But even as the bishop saves the man with the first touch of
grace Valjean has experienced, so does he ask something of the
stranger: "Do not forget, ever," he says, "that you have promised me
to use this silver to become an honest man."[2]

That Valjean, of course, never made such a promise only
underscores how the bishop looks not at who this man *is* but at
the redeemed man he *might be*. Valjean may not have made such
a promise, but the bishop imagines the new Valjean as capable of
doing so. "Jean Valjean, my brother, you no longer belong to evil

15

but good," he says. "It is your soul I am buying for you. I withdraw it from dark thoughts and from the spirit of perdition, and I give it to God."[3]

And yet, shortly after the interaction, Valjean steals a coin from Petit Gervais, a little boy who works as a chimney sweep. If it is an odd reaction to having just been showered with unforeseen grace, it seems a necessary, if subconscious, step for Valjean. Until now, he has seen the world as evil; he just finished serving a nineteen-year prison sentence for stealing a loaf of bread to serve his sister's hungry family. He has been turned away countless times as a free man. He can easily see the evil in the world.

But after he takes the chimney sweep's coin and looks at himself through the filter of the bishop's grace, he sees, for the first time, the evil in *himself*. He has stolen from someone even more defenseless than he. And yet something won't let Valjean remain mired in such selfishness. He recoils at his own evilness. Initially he tries to earn his way back to righteousness. He is all "works" and no "grace." He tries in vain to find the boy to return his coin. He gives money to the poor. He asks a priest to arrest him for robbery. "I'm such a miserable man!" he cries out.[4]

Then . . . it happens.

Jean Valjean breaks down into tears. He repents. His hardened heart finally grows soft—the kind of turnaround that can happen, not only in the imagination of a writer a long time ago, but in the hearts of people today.

I think back to a then-young man who, four decades ago, lived down the hall from me in my college dormitory. Not a copy-and-paste version of Jean Valjean, no, but a young man who shared with him a heart hardened to God. Not because of bitterness rooted in prison and injustice; no, quite the opposite. Because of pride rooted in wealth and entitlement.

He was a dashing, big-city boy—Myriel in his youth—who acted as if he were God's gift to our college town. Arrogant. Self-obsessed. And, you might think, echoing the words Javert sang to Jean Valjean in the musical version of *Les Misérables*: "Men like you can never change."[5]

Then . . . it happened.

He changed. Grace found him—not in a bishop's house but in the cab of an eighteen-wheeler driven by a man who welcomed in this college-aged hitchhiker. A candlestick conversion on Interstate 5. God's grace suddenly brought light to the darkness that, until then—until he got real with himself—he'd masked so well with bravado.

I saw him five years later at an Oregon beach town. He was a long-haired "Jesus freak" handing out tracts in the late 1970s. I saw him again ten years later, behind a desk in a suit, the pastor of one of our town's largest churches, hair shortly cropped. And I've seen him upon occasion since. I've seen his generosity toward others; he helped start a major food bank for our community's many homeless. I've seen his warmheartedness; his is a church that welcomes *les misérables.* And I've seen his clear understanding that it's not about him; gone is that smug self-righteousness with the blue-blood twist.

The fiction of nineteenth-century France. The truth of America today. The common denominator? Grace that—whoever we are, wherever we live, whatever we've done in the past—can melt the coldest heart.

Lesson 6

BLESSED ARE THE POOR IN SPIRIT

His cries died away into the mist, without even an echo.[1]
—HUGO, ON JEAN VALJEAN

THE THEME OF THE 1984 ADVERTISEMENT WAS SIMPLE: "NEVER let them see you sweat." It was for an antiperspirant, Dry Idea, and its point was that no matter how much pressure bore down on you, the best answer was keeping your cool. The football coach being grilled by the press. The comedian facing a tough crowd. The actress doing an early-morning audition. Above all, the ad suggested, keep your cool. We should be all about "maximum control."

After his encounters with the bishop and with the little boy, Petit Gervais, Jean Valjean is sweating profusely. In the span of a few hours, his once-staid life journey is pounding this way and that like a wild river. First, he encounters something he has never experienced before: grace. Then he answers such kindness with the stuff that sends men to prison: greed. He is all about "mini-mum control." The two incidents clash in his soul with such fervor that Valjean acts like a crazed man in his efforts to deal with the opposing forces: the forgiveness offered by the bishop and the futility of Valjean to find atonement for his subsequent theft.

Valjean tries desperately to deal with the dichotomy. As the moon rises in the darkness, "his cries died away into the mist, without even an echo." Finally, he is left mumbling the name of the little boy, so fully aware of his transgression that he is simultaneously driven to make things right and driven so mad that he can't. "That," writes Hugo, "was his last effort."[2]

He can do no more on his own. He is *It's a Wonderful Life*'s George Bailey standing on the bridge on Christmas Eve, thinking he has no place else to go. He is every person who has run and run and run from some situation, then, exhausted, given up. He is, at last, a man "poor in spirit" (Matt. 5:3).

"His knees suddenly bent under him," writes Hugo, "as if an invisible power suddenly overwhelmed him with the weight of his bad conscience; he fell exhausted onto a large rock, his hands clenched in his hair, and his face on his knees, and cried out, 'I'm such a miserable man!'"[3]

He is quite the opposite of the never-let-them-see-you-sweat folks; the embodiment not of maximum control but of minimal control. And, blessedly, right where God wants him: Poor in spirit. Humble. Broken. Pliable.

"Blessed are the poor in spirit," says Jesus, "for theirs is the kingdom of heaven" (Matt. 5:3).

C. S. Lewis writes, "St. Augustine says, 'God gives where He finds empty hands. A man whose hands are full of parcels can't receive a gift.'"[4]

Often the richer we are in *things*, the poorer we are in our *hearts.* Being poor in spirit is the deepest form of repentance because it acknowledges our desperate need for God. The rich, young ruler of Matthew 19:16–26 can't get there. Told to sell all he has, give to the poor, and follow Jesus, he goes away grieving, ultimately placing his faith in himself. The tax collector of Luke 18, on the other hand, *can* get there. "God," he says, "have mercy on me, a sinner" (v. 13).

Jean Valjean's brokenness triggers a flood of emotion. The irony? In losing control—in coming clean, being honest, and letting God and the whole world *see him sweat*—Jean Valjean is being real. Laid bare without pretense, he is allowing insight into his very soul. Valjean has faced "the beast" within, writes Hugo. "He could see his life, and it seemed horrible; his soul, and it seemed frightful."[5]

But Valjean's acceptance of his spiritual poverty—his humility—does not stymie him. On the contrary, it releases him. It sets him free. It unlocks dormant potential. "God opposes the proud," says James 4:6, "but gives grace to the humble."

If such an act requires pain, then it delivers promise. When the scales fall off our eyes, we see not only who we've been but more important—as did the bishop who exhorts Valjean to be an honest man—who we might be.

Nobody, Hugo writes, knew how long Jean Valjean wept or what he did afterward. We only know that at about 3:00 a.m., a stage driver arriving in Digne from Grenoble "saw a man kneeling in prayer, on the pavement in the dark, before the door of Monseigneur Bienvenu."[6]

Lesson 7

Actions trump words

He behaved the same with the rich as with the poor.[1]
—Hugo, regarding the bishop

What drives Jean Valjean to fall not only on bended knee but bended knee in front of the house of the man from whom he has stolen the silver? Why not somewhere else—a church, for example? Why not as far from the bishop's house as possible, to distance himself from his past?

Perhaps because this Monseigneur Bienvenu—Myriel—is the first one in Valjean's life not to beat him down but to lift him up. "Look down, look down. Don't look 'em in the eye," sings Valjean and the other prisoners in the musical's opening song.[2] But Myriel treats Valjean like a king. Javert, a prison guard, is quick to establish a we-they relationship to remind the prisoner that Javert is good (high) and Valjean is bad (low)—and should be looked down upon. But the bishop gives Valjean credence nobody else does. Meanwhile, at no point does Myriel point out to Valjean that he is "The Bishop." When Valjean says to him, "You are an innkeeper," Myriel says, "I am the priest who lives here." It is not until the next morning, when one of the officers refers to Myriel as "Monseigneur," that Valjean realizes the man not only isn't an innkeeper, a curé, or a priest, but is a member of the church's highest order of ministry.[3]

Perhaps Valjean returns to the bishop's house because Myriel is the first one in Valjean's life to speak of hope instead of hopelessness. Myriel treats Valjean as if the former convict is the embodiment of hope. As if he can be trusted. As if he is an honest man. "Go in peace," he says after the officers release Valjean. ". . . When you come again, you needn't come through the garden. You can always come and go by the front door."[4]

Such reasons might explain why Valjean kneels before the bishop's house; however, they don't explain his decision as well as this: because the kindness extended to Valjean in word on the night he arrived is reinforced to Valjean by deed on the morning he is apprehended by the police. In other words, what draws Valjean back is that Myriel walks the talk. He remains true to the kindhearted man he seems to be instead of succumbing to circumstances and turning his back on the obviously desperate man. In essence, he isn't the bane of Christianity today: a hypocrite.

Nothing lifts Jesus' message of hope more than those who live it out in the lives of others; nothing disparages it more than those who don't.

I was teaching a university reporting class when, after a few weeks, I realized one student seemed to loathe me. She argued about every grade I gave her. She exuded a body-language vibe that suggested I was the enemy. She talked me down in front of others. Finally, I asked her if she would stay after class.

"You don't seem to like me," I said.

"No, I don't."

"Have I done something to offend you?"

"You work at a newspaper—the liberal media—and you have fifteen of the sixteen students cowed," she said, "but not me."

Her perspective took me aback. Though certainly flawed, I'd been a believer for three decades, written faith-based books, and served on our nondenominational church's elder board. But to her, I was nothing more than an extension of what she saw as The Evil Empire.

"So," I said, deciding to play along with her perspective, "why aren't you 'cowed' like the others?"

"Because," she said with righteous indignation, "I'm a *Christian*."

Ouch. She used the word as if it were a knife meant to stab and twist: *Christian*.

I wanted to say, "Okay, let's just keep that our little secret." Instead, I could only lament how interactions like this one give credence to the "God, I Fear Your Followers" bumper stickers. Or the words of Gandhi: "I like your Christ. I do not like your Christians. They are so unlike your Christ." I could only imagine how, if I weren't a believer, her quick-to-judge attitude wouldn't have encouraged me to consider being one. I could only imagine how hypocrisy—saying one thing and doing another—grieves God.

Valjean later faces the prospect of hypocrisy when he wrestles with whether to come clean in court regarding a man claiming to be him. He rationalizes that to stay silent might be wise, even if it means injustice for the other man. Then he catches himself. "It was," Hugo writes, "the last hypocritical wrong."[5]

The reason Victor Hugo could relate, perhaps, was that in his own life hypocrisy dogged him with the persistence of Javert, even if his adoring followers overlooked it: he wrote glowingly of integrity but betrayed the trust of his wife; he fanned the virtues of self-sacrifice but honed a legendary sense of personal vanity; he trumpeted a gospel as clear as a mountain stream but dabbled in the occult.

"Do not merely listen to the word, and so deceive yourselves," says James 1:22. "Do what it says."

Saying, "I'm a Christian" in defense of mistreating another is like saying, "I'm a vegetarian" while wolfing down a Big Mac. Alas, you don't have to look far to see such hypocrisy among those who've linked their lives—or at least *say* they've linked their lives—to Jesus. You see it in the basketball coach at the Christian school whose reputation around the league is as the biggest foot-stomping, ref-baiting, player-bashing one of the bunch. In the church elder whose reputation in the business community is of a swindler. In the televangelist who preaches all the love-the-poor stuff but sells his $2.9 million mansion so he can move into a $10.5 million mansion. (Were there to be a knock on *his* door late one night, the guest would probably not be allowed in as Valjean was. Instead, the security staff might be fired on the spot for allowing the intrusion.)

Today, social media gives us more temptations to twist the truth on who we really are. To hide our dark sides and ballyhoo the light. In essence, to be who we'd like people to think we are and not necessarily who we really are. But what resonates with people is those who say one thing and do that one thing. In the case of the bishop, a man who comes across as humble, giving, and noble—and when put to the test, proves to be humble, giving, and noble. Valjean returns to the bishop's house on bended knee because he realizes the man is the real deal. He not only says he cares, he proves he cares with his actions.

In other words, sometimes the best sermon isn't a sermon. Writes Hugo, through the eyes of the bishop's sister, who witnessed the interaction: "It was certainly a golden opportunity to get in a little sermon and to set the bishop above the convict in order to make an impression on his mind."[6]

Suggesting she is cut from the same cloth as her brother, the woman later writes, "Isn't there . . . something truly evangelical in this tact, which refrains from sermonizing, moralizing, and making illusions? Isn't it most sympathetic, when a man has a bruise, not to touch it at all?"[7]

So, instead, the bishop offers bread, wine, warmth, compassion, and encouragement, tying the package securely the next morning with grace to confirm the worth of his words.

As Saint Francis of Assisi is believed to have said, "Preach the gospel at all times. If necessary, use words."

Lesson 8

It's not about "the stuff"

*They confuse heaven's radiant stars with a
duck's footprint left in the mud.*[1]

—LES MISÉRABLES

AFTER JEAN VALJEAN LEAVES WITH THE BISHOP'S SILVER—AND
before he is apprehended by the police and returned—Myriel's
servant reacts with told-you-so anger. "The wretch!" she says. "He
stole our silver!"[2]

The bishop's response is telling. "Now first," he says, "did this
silver belong to us?" As a disbelieving Madame Magloire listens, he
adds a sort of Mother Teresa spin to the whole situation: "For a long
time I have wrongfully been withholding this silver. It belonged to
the poor. Who was this man? A poor man, quite clearly."[3]

When a chagrined Madame Magloire worries aloud about
what the bishop will eat with now, he gently puts into perspective
the insignificance of the material. Pewter cutlery will do, he says.
When Madame Magloire counters that pewter smells, he suggests
iron. It has a taste, she says. "Well, then," says the bishop, "wooden
implements."[4]

He is saying that what we eat with matters little—or should matter little; deeper things are at work here than silver, pewter, and iron. Myriel, obviously, is far more concerned about Jean Valjean's fate. He is clearly a Matthew 6:20–21 guy who understands life isn't about "the stuff" down here but eternity beyond.

"But store up for yourselves treasures in heaven, where moths and vermin do not destroy, and where thieves do not break in and steal," says the passage. "For where your treasure is, there your heart will be also."

On the opposite side of the equation, some people worship so vainly the idols of money, stuff, and experiences—the material—that they overlook the deeper virtues beyond. It reminds me of a television show I came across called *Four Weddings*, in which soon-to-be brides assess one another's weddings, and the one who accumulates the most points wins a honeymoon trip with her new husband. The weddings, some of which run north of fifty thousand dollars, come across as lavish cocktail parties with a couple of "I do" vows thrown in for good measure. One bride, assessing another's wedding, complained that the bar didn't serve tequila shots, another that the wedding dress didn't do enough to hide the bride's pregnancy, a third that the seafood fondue was cold.

It all represents a feast of the trivial and a famine of the significant, as if the marriage to follow is only a bit player in this high-emotion drama. That's what seems to get lost in a materialistic world, not simply excess for excess's sake, but the profundity that is overlooked in the process.

The problem with eating junk food—and, believe me, I'm the poster boy for this weakness—isn't only the bad stuff we inject in our bodies; it's the good stuff we ignore in so doing. When we slip into the narcissistic worship of stuff—i.e., self—we lose focus on those around us in need. When we shop for our contentment instead of trusting in God's promises, we, like the four brides, have forgotten that it's the marriage, not the wedding, that deserves our time and attention.

We like to point the finger at the materialism of the wealthy; it conveniently points the finger away from those of us who aren't rich. And yet the malady is an equal-opportunity masquerader of true meaning, afflicting rich and poor. Consider, for example, the spartan existence lived by the bishop's servant, Madame Magloire. She has little and yet, unlike the bishop, worries not about the soul of an obviously troubled man but about the composition of eating implements.

When we cling too tightly to "stuff," we major in the minors and minor in the majors. I was parking cars for a wedding of a friend's son. My instructions were to send the first few dozen cars to a gravel lot to leave the choicer, paved spots for late-arriving guests. But one man flat-out refused and insisted on parking on the pavement. He was driving a BMW. "He doesn't want to get it dinged on the gravel," his wife said with a sheen of apology. *Really? Three miles per hour on a gravel parking lot?* As he drove by, I said to myself, "That car means way too much to that guy."

Hugo writes that we have "confused heaven's radiant stars with a duck's footprint left in the mud,"[5] the inference being that the solution begins with perspective. Better to look up and realize that stuff is just that, *stuff*—and that, in the end, he who dies with the most of it still dies. Better to search for contentment on a higher plane by looking up to heaven's radiant stars.

THE CONSCIENCE MUST
NOT BE IGNORED

One can no more keep the mind from returning to an
idea than the sea from returning to a shore. For the sailor,
this is called the tide; in the case of the guilty, it is called
remorse. God stirs up the soul as well as the ocean.[1]
—LES MISÉRABLES

IN 1815, A STRANGER COMES INTO MONTREUIL-SUR-MER, JUST east of Paris, and soon wins the affections of the community. He goes by the name of Monsieur Madeleine, though he used to go by Jean Valjean. He has invented a newer, cheaper method for producing black beads, the town's largest industry. He buys the factory. He is a bit peculiar—there was the time he dressed in black after the death of a bishop named Myriel—but seems honest, kind, and noble. He saves two local children from a fire. He gives freely to the poor. Within five years, he is appointed mayor. People, writes Hugo, would say of Madeleine: "There is a rich man who does not show pride."[2]

The only person in town who opposes Madeleine—Monsieur

le Maire (mayor) in the musical—is a man named Fauchelevent, whose slipping financial well-being clashes with Madeleine's rising good fortune; in short, he is jealous of the mayor. But one day Fauchelevent's cart breaks and pins him to the ground. Madeleine hurriedly offers money to anyone who will help the man. Nobody, including the town's police inspector, Javert, steps forward.

"Monsieur Madeleine," says Javert, "I have never known but one man capable of doing what you ask . . . He was a convict."[3]

Clearly Javert suspecs what Hugo has freely told the reader: Madeleine is, indeed, the former Jean Valjean and has broken his parole. If Madeleine frees Fauchelevent, he further risks Javert confirming the former convict's true identity. Madeleine's decision boils down to whose life is more important: his or that of a man who despises him.

He frees the man from beneath the cart. Later, in a separate incident, Javert demands that Madeleine relieve him of his duties because Javert had committed what he sees as an unpardonable transgression: accusing Madeleine of being the ex-convict Jean Valjean. But the real Valjean, he insists, has been found: a man soon to stand trial for stealing apples and who goes by the name Champmathieu, but whom Javert and three witnesses are certain is actually Jean Valjean.

In short, Madeleine suddenly has a perfect "out." All the real Jean Valjean has to do is look the other way, and Javert will be off his tail while a man he does not even know will conveniently take Valjean's identity to prison. And, he rationalizes, it will be for the good of the people: if Madeleine reveals his true identity, Champmathieu will be freed, but Madeleine will be imprisoned and no longer able to run the factory and help the poor—including

Fantine, a young woman he's discovered to be in desperate need. The temptation for Valjean is not to look down or to look up, but to look the other way.

Valjean refuses to accept Javert's resignation, but then he is faced with another dilemma: Should he turn himself in as the real Jean Valjean? Hugo spends eighty-two pages detailing Madeleine's agony over the decision. "Of all the things God has made," he writes, "the human heart is the one that sheds most light, and alas! most night."[4]

In his home, Madeleine senses he is not alone. "It seemed to him that somebody could see him," writes Hugo. "Who? Alas! . . . What he wanted to blind was looking at him. His conscience. His conscience, or God."[5]

To free himself is to condemn another. To rob an innocent, if deranged, man of "his life, his peace, his place in the world." To break his unspoken promise with the bishop to live an honest life. For the first time in eight years, since he stole from the young chimney sweep, after his encounter with the bishop, writes Hugo, "the unhappy man had just tasted the bitter flavor of a wicked thought and a wicked action. He spit it out with disgust."[6]

In the end, Madeleine listens to his conscience, listens to the bishop, listens, in essence, to God. "How could I ever face myself again?" he asks himself, the pivotal question whose answer becomes his decision.

"Release the accused," he tells the jury. "Your honor, order my arrest. He is not the man you seek; I am. I am Jean Valjean."[7]

In the cases of Fauchelevent and Champmathieu, Jean Valjean saves two men despite knowing that to do so will be detrimental to himself. For him, integrity trumps consequences. God trumps man. "Men could see his mask," writes Hugo, "but the bishop saw his face . . . Men saw his life, but the bishop saw his conscience."[8] As Hugo's extension of God, the bishop is Valjean's beacon of Proverbs 12:22: "The LORD detests lying lips, but he delights in people who are trustworthy."

It's convenient to consider lying, cheating, and stealing as the stuff of convicts and misfits. Prepare to feel inconvenienced: An estimated 1.6 million people cheat on their taxes, according to a 2013 Pew Research study, swiping $270 billion from all of us.[9] And in a survey conducted by the Los Angeles-based Josephson Institute, 64 percent of students at randomly selected high schools nationwide (public and private) had cheated on a test.[10]

Behavioral economist Dan Ariely, author of *The (Honest) Truth About Dishonesty*, said a few people are always honest, a few are never honest, and most live in the broad middle. "For most of us, the biggest driver of dishonesty is the ability to rationalize our actions so that we don't lose the sense of ourselves as good people," he said.[11]

In other words, such thinking goes, what's bad is *feeling bad about dishonesty*; dishonesty on its own is not. A dishonest action isn't bad as long as we can rationalize it as being appropriate. If-it-feels-good-do-it thinking always seems so practical—unless, of course, it's *our* houses or cars that get broken into by a thug for whom it "felt good."

For Jean Valjean, it is never about feelings. It is about following a conscience that demands honesty—a path we, too, should follow.

STARTING OVER CAN
REDEFINE OUR PURPOSE

Another story must begin![1]

—JEAN VALJEAN IN THE MUSICAL'S
SONG "VALJEAN'S SOLILOQUY"

THE CONVICT-TO-MAYOR, THIEF-TO-PHILANTHROPIST, TAKER-to-giver transformation of Jean Valjean is dramatic but real. In less than a decade, the man emerges as someone so totally different that you wouldn't think it possible.

"When he walked through a village the ragged little youngsters would run after him with joy and surround him like a swarm of flies," writes Hugo of the new Valjean.[2] A man who once sardonically suggested to the bishop that he might just murder him now strolled down the street with children following like pilot fish behind a ship.

Jean Valjean has changed not only his name but his entire approach to life. His purpose of living has changed, from self-preservation to serving others. In short, he has reinvented himself. Just as the bishop encouraged him to do, he sees in his redemption "some higher plan":[3] others. The workers in his factory. The children in his town.

In the musical version of *Les Misérables*, the "At the End of the Day" song speaks to a lack of purpose among the poor. The people are stuck in a grind; life lacks purpose centered on others.

But lack of purpose isn't confined to the poor. Jack Tripp gave up the good life on the East Coast to become executive director of a mission in the midsized West Coast community where I live. Why? Because, he told me in an interview, he longed to live for something more than money and things.[4]

Tripp had been a self-described yuppie. Undergraduate degree in marketing. MBA from New York University. Management positions with Fortune 500 companies in New York, Singapore, Hong Kong, and Beijing. He owned a summer home on Cape Cod. Drove a BMW. Met his wife at the largest singles bar in Manhattan.

And a few years later, he was running a mission in Eugene, Oregon. He was spending a night, incognito, with the men in the sleeping room so he could gain perspective on what improvements needed to be made. He was revamping the entire nonprofit so it wasn't just a place to keep people alive on a cold winter's night, but was equipping them to leave the mission, get a job, and start *living*.

Like Jean Valjean, he'd gone from a grind without purpose to a life with renewed purpose. "Zero regrets," he said about this new life. "In my old world, you worked your head off, and the payoff was a bonus. Here, you work your head off but the payoff is seeing some guy who is riddled with heroin come through and a month later, give you a hug and say, 'Thanks. You helped save my life.'"[5]

Sometimes it pays to reinvent ourselves. "If you are in love," writes Oswald Chambers, "you do not sit down and dream about the one you love all the time, you go and do something for him."[6]

Valjean gets up and goes. Tripp got up and went.

We need to get up and go—sometimes by redefining who we are.

Goodness requires no audience

He did a multitude of good deeds as secretly
as bad ones are usually done.[1]

—Hugo, on Valjean

The goodness that Valjean-turned-Madeleine does in Montreuil-sur-Mer goes on and on. He embraces the bereavement of others, seeks out funerals to attend, that he might encourage those in mourning. He makes sure ten new beds are added to the hospital. He pays teachers out of his own pocket. He teaches peasants how to better cultivate crops. He establishes a home for old and infirm laborers—on his own nickel, er, franc.

He does all this while seeking no credit for his good deeds. Indeed, he is so intent on spreading goodness without taking credit that—and I'm not endorsing this, by the way—he breaks into people's houses not to steal, but to leave "a piece of gold."[2]

We live in a world where people too often go out of their way to do good *just so they will be noticed.* The goodness becomes a means to an end, a personal public relations ploy. As a newspaper columnist, my favorite stories are about people who don't pine for the spotlight but who deserve it. But I am often contacted by people who may, indeed, "do unto others," but who desperately want the world to know about it.

Jesus, on the other hand, heals a blind man at Bethsaida and charges people to "not to tell anyone about him" (Mark 8:30).

He chastises the Pharisees for being hypocrites "who love to pray standing in the synagogues and on the street corners to be seen by others" (Matt. 6:5).

Why are we to do good? Because it glorifies God. Because it's the right thing to do. Because it's more blessed to give than to receive.

A reason *not* to do good? To be noticed.

"Be careful," says Jesus in Matthew 6, "not to do your 'acts of righteousness' before men, to be seen by them. If you do, you have no reward from your Father in heaven. So when you give to the needy, do not announce it with trumpets, as the hypocrites do in the synagogues and on the streets, to be honored by men" (vv. 1–2).

In *Les Misérables*, Jean Valjean saves at least nine people: two children in Montreuil-sur-Mer from a fire; Fauchelevent from being crushed to death by a cart; Cosette from her troubled life with the Thénardiers; Fantine from being sent to prison; Champmathieu from returning to prison; a sailor in Toulon from almost certain death; Javert from death after Enjolras commands Valjean to execute the spy; and Marius from probable execution by the approaching army.

But he never does so for his own personal glory. Like him, we must be about the deed, not the credit. About the heart, not the headlines.

When our church partnered with an organization to feed

the poor recently, I was puzzled by something I saw after the food had been prepared and the line of people started to move through. The first person through was not one of the homeless people we were serving but the director of the operation. And he was heaping huge mounds of food on the plate he carried.

If this event were being done in the name of Jesus, who washed His disciples' feet, wasn't it a bit hypocritical for the leader to go first, to bask in a touch of look-at-me glory?

Then I came closer. The new perspective helped me see the whole picture. There, behind the director, was a tattered man in a wheelchair.

The director was preparing the heaping plate for him.

Lesson 12

OUR ACTIONS RIPPLE THROUGH TIME

Each time the priest uttered the word "Monsieur" in his mild, companionable voice the man's face lighted up. The courtesy, to the ex-convict, was like fresh water to a shipwrecked man.[1]

—HUGO, ON MYRIEL

FANTINE, WRITES HUGO, IS AN "ANONYMOUS" SOUL, BEAUTI-ful but abandoned, having never known a mother or father, "an infant wandering barefoot in the streets."[2] At fifteen, never having felt the security of familial love, she moves to Paris, where, as a seamstress in 1817, she falls for a student, Félix Tholomyès.

He is wealthy. Insecure. Arrogant. "To him," writes Hugo, "it was an affair; to her a passion."[3] A way to believe she is loved. A way to feel secure. A way to compensate for all she has never been given.

Alas, Tholomyès sees her as nothing more than a play toy. After two years, he, along with three friends courting friends of Fantine's, concocts a cruel surprise for the four women. The young men are being summoned by their parents to return home. So, in a two-birds-with-one-stone gesture, they invite the four women to a plush dinner and leave under the guise of soon returning, but instead have their waiter take the women a letter that offers a smarmy good-bye. The relationships are over. They are going home: "For nearly two years we have made you happy. Bear us no ill will for it . . . P.S. The dinner is paid for."[4]

Like the others, Fantine laughs at first at what the men saw as a good joke, even if their intent was, indeed, to abandon the women. But later, alone, she weeps. "She had given herself to Tholomyès as to a husband, and the poor girl had his child."[5] His love-her-and-leave-her decision sends Fantine on a trajectory toward tragedy.

Even if he never realizes the ramifications of his actions, you can argue that Tholomyès's gutless abandoning of the pregnant young woman ultimately costs Fantine her life—and, were it not for Jean Valjean's intervention, would have condemned her daughter, Cosette, to a similar fate.

Granted, Fantine went into the relationship with her eyes open. But if it takes two to tango, it takes only one to deceive. In this case, Tholomyès. Perhaps pulling similar pranks on other unsuspecting women, as Hugo suggests, he went blissfully on with his life. Fantine does not go blissfully on with hers, sinking into poverty, prostitution, and humiliation. As she sings in "I Dreamed a Dream": "I had a dream my life would be so different from this hell I'm living."[6]

Would Fantine have been in this position had Tholomyès not initially betrayed her? Not likely. She would have been with her daughter, where a mother belongs, and probably would not have slipped into the poverty and pain that leads to her death. But, years after Tholomyès's cruel departure, his ripples of irresponsibility build into a wave of desperation for Fantine that kills her—even as, Hugo points out, he goes on to become "a fat provincial attorney, rich and influential, a wise voter and rigid juror, but as always, a man of pleasure."[7]

Our actions affect people—for better or worse. It's not always comfortable considering the latter, but we must.

When I was in elementary school, a classmate of mine whose parents had died was so desperate for friends that he offered me a dollar to play two square with him. It grieves me to admit it, but I accepted. Decades later, when he was middle-aged, I heard he had committed suicide. And I was left wondering: Was I—if even in a small, indirect way—an accomplice to his death?

It's easy, of course, to argue away such a notion; that the two-square episode was a small incident forty years ago. I have no idea why he decided to take his life; it may well have been nothing related to childhood scars that masked wounds of loneliness so deep that he might, in essence, pay someone to be his friend for recess. But if others, throughout his life, humiliated him as I did by affirming his desperation—if few were willing to affirm him with friendship—you can understand why someone might wonder about the value of his life. And to completely dismiss the possibility of a connection is to overlook how we affect others.

Fantine's progression toward death—she develops a chronic chest condition—involves myriad circumstances, choices, and people; it occurs over many years' time and is hastened by an incident where a "customer" stuffs snow down her back. And yet what triggers her descent is one man's selfish decision, without which these other factors may have never come into play. Likewise, what triggered my classmate's descent could have been a series of events like the one on the playground, each person's acceptance of his pay-to-play offer sending him deeper into a subconscious sense of worthlessness.

How differently might his life have turned out had I—and others in similar positions—just said, "Forget the buck. Let's play two square." If, along with others, I had befriended him instead of, in a sense, betrayed him.

I've written seventeen books. When people ask what led me to become a writer, I'm quick to point to a handful of people in my early years who believed in me. I'm quick to credit incremental encouragement that began building a sense in me that, as a writer, I could succeed. By the same token, is it so far-fetched to believe that people who struggle in life do so at least in part because of people in their early years who did *not* believe in them? Who did *not* encourage them? Who gradually built in them a sense that they could *not* succeed?

Granted, at the end of the day we're each responsible for our choices; some people too easily play the victim card. But that doesn't absolve us from also taking responsibility for how we treat others, even in seemingly small ways.

"Hugo's gift to the people simultaneously affirms that every citizen is important to the health of the nation and emphasizes how that fact gives each individual responsibility for the conditions we all share," says a Penguin.com essay on the movie. "Hugo sees the world as a convoluted pattern: '*Nothing is truly small . . . within that inexhaustible compass, from the sun to the grub, there is no room for disdain; each thing needs every other thing.*' He illustrates a system full of injustice, but in that same sphere, a single gesture of kindness redeems the world."[8]

Connecting the dots of how we affect the world around us can be a guilt-producing business, I realize. And yet it would be callous to dismiss Hugo's idea that "great blunders are often made, like large ropes, of a multitude of fibers."[9]

We dare not ignore the reality that our interactions with others matter, now and beyond.

Lesson 13

WE NEED TO SEE PEOPLE AS GOD SEES PEOPLE

*For prying into other people's affairs, none are
equal to those of whom it is no concern.[1]*

—*LES MISÉRABLES*

IN THE BEAD FACTORY, A COWORKER STEALS A LETTER OF Fantine's from the Thénardiers regarding Cosette. Word spreads. The young woman has a child out of wedlock, which whips her fellow workers into an anti-Fantine fervor. Whatever their motives—jealousy, pride, something to forget their own sad lives—the other women at the factory peck at Fantine like crows thrown crumbs of bread. "A sad thing," writes Hugo.[2]

They milk the "bastard child" gossip for all it is worth. In the musical, the uproar turns into a physical tussle between Fantine and the unspoken leader of the gossip birds. In the 2012 movie version, Madeleine intervenes, telling his foreman to handle it— and to "be as patient as you can."[3] Moments later, the foreman throws Fantine into the street, a convenient way for him to vent his frustration at her for deflecting his implied sexual advances. If the book version lacks the emotion of the musical scene, Fantine is, in Hugo's version, nevertheless fired on the spot for having a child out of wedlock.

This makes Madeleine's defense of Fantine in a subsequent incident seem all the more remarkable. On the street, Fantine has a run-in with Bamatabois, a Tholomyès-like man who preys on her weakness. When Bamatabois's taunts become physical—he throws snow down her back—she lashes back at him. Javert, the police inspector, arrives on the scene and—without need for a judge or jury—tells her she is headed for six months in jail.

Enter Monsieur Madeleine, who sees her as less of a trouble-maker than a victim. If her fellow factory workers see the worst in Fantine, Madeleine sees the best—even after she thanks him for intervening by spitting in Madeleine's face, convinced that it was his recommendation to the factory foreman that had her fired. But Madeleine doesn't let that deter him. "Set this woman free," he tells Javert.[4]

When, in the book version, she begins telling of the wretched treatment prisoners receive in jail, Madeleine doesn't scold her. He listens. Javert does not. When she walks toward the door, Javert says to a sergeant, "Don't you see that this tramp is escaping . . . this wretched woman has insulted a citizen."

Madeleine defends the "wretched woman" and, in so doing, risks offending the town's highly respected police inspector. "I heard everything," he says. "It is the citizen who is in the wrong; it is he who, with proper police work, should have been arrested."[5]

As Javert continues to protest, Madeleine cites his mayoral authority in such matters and tells Fantine, "You may go."[6] As with animals who've been caged for a long time, she is loath to leave. Dazed. Not unlike Jean Valjean when the bishop sets him free, for Fantine, like him, has never known human grace until this moment. She is like a coal miner trapped beneath the earth who sees the sky again, initially blinded by the light.

"Before her eyes she had seen a struggle between two men who held in their hands her liberty, her life, her soul, her child," writes Hugo. "One of these men was drawing her to the side of darkness, the other was leading her toward the light."[7]

When the two are alone, Madeleine tells Fantine he did not know she had been fired. He insists he will pay her debts. He tells her he will care for her and her child, Cosette.

"I do not doubt it," he says, "that you have never ceased to be virtuous and holy before God. Poor woman."[8]

Again, the similarities are telling between the bishop seeing the promise in Jean Valjean and the ex-convict seeing the promise in Fantine, as if the latter incident has been born of the former. Madeleine's seeing of the good in Fantine only underscores how quickly her fellow factory workers were to see the worst. Though we might wish otherwise, sometimes we play the part of Fantine's fellow factory workers. "The average Christian," writes Oswald Chambers, "is the most penetratingly critical individual."[9]

Madeleine intervenes in a volatile situation and brings peace. The factory workers turn a peaceful atmosphere into one of contention, all for the thrill of stirring up trouble. "Without wood a fire goes out; without a gossip a quarrel dies down," says Proverbs 26. "As charcoal to embers and as wood to fire, so is a quarrelsome person for kindling strife. The words of a gossip are like choice morsels; they go down to the inmost parts" (vv. 20–22).

And words of praise? "Sociologists have a theory of the looking-glass self," writes Philip Yancey in *What's So Amazing About Grace?* "You become what the most important person in your life (wife, father, boss, etc.) thinks you are. How would my life change if I truly believed the Bible's astounding words about God's love for me, if I looked in the mirror and saw what God sees?"[10]

Likewise, how would our lives change if we saw others as God sees them? "Here lies hidden the great call to conversion," writes Nouwen. "To look not with the eyes of my own low self-esteem, but with the eyes of God's love."[11]

We need to see others not through our egocentric filters, but through the same God-centered perspective that allows the bishop to see the potential in Jean Valjean and Valjean the potential in Fantine.

CRISIS REVEALS
CHARACTER

Adversity makes men, and prosperity makes monsters.
—VICTOR HUGO

BAMATABOIS, WRITES HUGO, IS NOT UNLIKE THOLOMYÈS, who had gotten Fantine pregnant and then left her. A "provincial dandy," writes Hugo of the man who confronts Fantine after she's been fired from the factory. He doesn't even aspire to a good pickup line. Instead, he says to her, "My, but you're ugly. Why don't you try hiding your face?"[1]

When Fantine retaliates, Javert arrests and sentences her to jail. The woman becomes like the basketball player who is whistled for a "retaliation foul," when the referee misses the real injustice and only sees the payback. Context, as we will learn, is not Javert's strong suit.

At the police station, she is being carted away when Madeleine arrives. Somehow he has heard of the incident and has come to pardon Fantine. To undo what Javert has done. To set her free. (Based, we're told, on a true story in which Hugo saved a wronged girl from a certain prison sentence by telling police they should have arrested the man, not her.)

Crisis always reveals character. And that's what we're seeing here, someone not afraid of getting involved.

When calamity reigns, how do we react? Do we intervene in the name of justice, or do we run—or, more likely, quietly excuse ourselves, lest we be noticed for our lack of courage? Do we assume things will work out, or do we do whatever we can to help?

Getting involved means risk, vulnerability, and, at the very least, inconvenience. How many times have I seen an incident and instead of stepping in to help, assumed someone else would? The person on the side of the road with a flat. (*Someone else will stop.*) The man at church who, in my post-service chat, mentions, again, that he is unable to find work. (*Someone else will give him money or pray for him on the spot.*) The woman who, in a coastal town where I led a recent writers' conference, walks down the road, deliriously screaming, "Don't leave me! Don't leave me!" (*Someone else will intervene and help her with whatever demons she's dealing with—or she'll solve the dilemma on her own.*)

In this case, the woman, I later learned, "solved her dilemma" by beating up someone in a bar a few minutes later, stealing the keys to her boyfriend's car, racing through the small town at speeds estimated up to sixty miles per hour—narrowly missing a car with a family in it—and sailing off a cliff and onto the surf-splashed rocks below.

She survived. But in retrospect, I should have intervened. Yes, hindsight is 20/20. And no, I had no inkling what was about to come. But, given a replay on that scene, I should have tried to help her. Might she have refused that help, given her state of mind?

Sure. Still, if she were my daughter-in-law or my wife, I would have wanted someone to help save her from herself.

Can things go wrong when we intervene? Yes. A friend of mine loaned tools to a down-and-out guy looking for help, and the guy stole them. It happens. But, on my deathbed, I'd rather look back and realize I lost a few tools than that I never reached out to someone in need. I honor my friend for what he did because it reflects heart, not stupidity.

When my father died, my wife and I rushed to the mountain resort where he and other family members had been staying at the time. I comforted my mother. But the real hero was my wife, who immediately took charge of cleaning up the room where he'd died of congestive heart failure, where emergency personnel had just been, where my mother didn't need to be. In such moments, there's no time to think about getting credit or looking good in front of others; you just do what needs to be done.

Plain and simple, crisis reveals character.

Lesson 15

GRACE, ACCEPTED, CHANGES US

I have been a sinner, but when I have my child with me that will mean God has forgiven me.[1]

—FANTINE

IN THE BLINK OF AN EYE, FANTINE GOES FROM CALLOUSED lady of the night—even if not by choice—to gentle angel of the infirmary. Why? Grace, pure and simple.

Madeleine's intervention and his offer to help melts her heart, gives her hope, and soothes her anger. To understand her darkness before he bathes her in light, you need only to read Hugo's description of her retaliation on the cad who stuffed snow down her back: "The girl roared in rage, turned, bounded like a panther, and rushed at the man, burying her nails in his face, and using the most shocking words, usually heard only in the barracks. These insults were thrown out in a voice roughened by brandy, from a hideous mouth minus two front teeth."[2]

In that moment, it is as if all her betrayals well up in a single act of anger, frustration, and defiance: Tholomyès abandoning her, her coworkers turning on her, the foreman firing her, men—with her tepid consent—having their way with her, and God—at least in her eyes—condemning her. In the musical she sings of her dream "that God would be forgiving."[3]

Now, all that she'd hoped for is gone; the icy snowball down the back is the final humiliation for a young woman who is physically sick and emotionally empty, who has lost her teeth, her hair, her pride, and her hope. And yet, in the infirmary, soon after she's been saved by Madeleine's extension of grace, Fantine "stretched her hands toward heaven, and the expression on her face became indescribable. Her lips move; she is praying in a whisper. When her prayer ends, 'My sisters,' she says to the nuns, 'I'm quite willing to lie down again, I'll do whatever you say; I was wrong just now, pardon me for having talked so loud; it's bad to talk so loud; I know it, my good sister, but you see I'm so happy. God is kind, Monsieur Madeleine is good; just think of it, that he has gone to Montfermeil for my little Cosette.'"[4]

Grace, pure and simple.

"I do not understand the mystery of grace," writes author Anne Lamott in *Traveling Mercies: Some Thoughts on Faith*, "only that it meets us where we are and does not leave us where it found us."[5]

"The world can do almost anything as well as or better than the church," says author Gordon MacDonald. "You need not be a Christian to build houses, feed the hungry, or heal the sick. There is only one thing the world cannot do. It cannot offer grace."[6]

But, powered by God, we can—if we choose to.

The biggest dichotomy in the church today is that two people can be sitting next to each other, ostensibly believe essentially the same things about God, hear the same sermon, and sing the same songs—and yet, when the service is over, go into the world with totally different dispositions, perspectives, and motives. One will forgive his or her detractors, feed the poor, and look for the promise in people; the other will hold grudges, look at a street-corner beggar with disgust not compassion, and assess others through an eye of self-righteousness and conceit.

Writes counselor David Seamands:

> Many years ago I was driven to the conclusion that the two major causes of most emotional problems among evangelical Christians are these: the failure to understand, receive, and live out God's unconditional grace and forgiveness; and the failure to give out that unconditional love, forgiveness, and grace to other people . . . We read, we hear, we believe a good theology of grace. But that's not what we live. The good news of the Gospel of grace has not penetrated the level of our emotions.[7]

And yet, here is Fantine, changed. By what? A warm bed, sure. Safety? Sure. Nuns waiting on her? Sure. The hope of being reunited with her daughter? Sure. All these things, yes, but combined, they are not able to soften a hardened heart like Madeleine offering her mercy that the law suggests she does not deserve.

The law—aka Javert—says *punishment*. Six months in jail, where people go to rot. The law is salt in already-painful wounds.

Grace—aka Valjean—says *forgiveness*. An infirmary, where people go to heal. Grace is salve to a wounded soul.

"The world thirsts for grace in ways it does not even recognize," writes Yancey.[8]

And so it is that Fantine, if even on her deathbed, thirsts no more.

Our strengths can become our weaknesses

*[Javert] had nothing but disdain, aversion, and disgust for
all who had once overstepped the bounds of the law.[1]*

—Les Misérables

IF YOU LOOK STRICTLY AT HIS RÉSUMÉ, YOU CAN ALMOST LIKE
Javert, the police inspector. Born to a gypsy in prison, he has pulled
himself up by his bootstraps to become a highly respected officer. Right is right. Wrong is wrong. Integrity matters. Conscience
matters. Honor matters. Above all, the law matters.

His instincts are good. He suspects—rightly so as it turns
out—that Madeleine might be Jean Valjean. But when he learns
of a slightly deranged prisoner confessing to being Jean Valjean,
Javert is so racked with shame for having suspected Madeleine that
he offers his own resignation, though Valjean pardons him. Such
is the strength of the man, a willingness to adhere so tightly to the
law that he would call out even himself when thinking that the law
has been violated.

Alas, the weakness of the man—like the law itself—is his

neglect of heart, of grace, of the human context that colors a crime or supposed crime. He looks at Jean Valjean and does not see a man, but Prisoner No. 24,601. And so it is that when Fantine lashes back at Bamatabois, Javert demands she be sent to prison. (As we have seen, Madeleine overrides his decision and lets her go free.) When Fauchelevent is being crushed beneath a wagon, Javert does send for a jack but shows far more suspicion about Madeleine's true identity than he does concern for the man being crushed. (Again, Madeleine literally takes matters into his own hands and lifts the cart himself.) And when Fantine lies dying, Javert calls her a "whore," derides a town "where convicts are magistrates and prostitutes are nursed like countesses," and refuses Valjean's plea to give him three days so he can "go for the child of this unhappy woman," instead arresting him on the spot.[2] (Madeleine worries about the well-being of the now-orphaned Cosette.)

In Javert's world there are only good guys and bad guys: those who uphold the law and those who attack it. He never understands that the mass of humanity lives somewhere in between.

In Hugo's time and place, law with no grace begets a heartless world in which women are all but forced to sell their bodies to survive, then are punished for doing so. Law with no context sends a man to prison for stealing a loaf of bread to save his starving family. Law with no respect for human beings turns those incarcerated into animals.

The lesson for us: our greatest strengths become our greatest weaknesses when left unchecked. Though Javert's toe-the-line mentality is often appropriate and admirable, it becomes a millstone for him—and society at large—when used without restraint. Without grace. Without a sense of humanity.

Marius, who falls in love with Cosette, redefines his life at one point with a newfound dedication to Napoleonism, but in so doing, becomes like a runaway cart on a downhill road. "Like all new converts to religion," writes Hugo, "his conversion intoxicated him, he plunged headlong into adhesion, and he went too far."[3]

I can relate. I tend to be passionate about whatever I do. But when disunity fractured our church long ago, I went too far with passionate words in trying to right what I saw as a wrong. When discussing something with my wife, I can go too far in trying to "editorialize" my point of view instead of listening to her. When organizing an extended-family outing, I can quickly become like Robert DeNiro's portrayal of the father in *Meet the Parents*: so regimented in my attempt to make sure we all have a good time that nobody has a good time.

Notching back the passionate pursuit of right doesn't mean neglecting justice. It means a heightened awareness for people, something we experienced recently in our community. Police officers, we learned, were buying sleeping bags for the homeless—with their own nickels.

Javert would have cringed, perhaps had the officers reprimanded, suspended, or fired.

We should applaud.

Trust can be misplaced

*You'll find a purse there and a watch. Take
them . . . You've saved my life.*[1]

—Colonel Georges Pontmercy, to Thénardier

On the battlefield at Waterloo, in 1815, what catches
the eye of a soldier named Thénardier is not the corpses lying in
frozen anguish. No, it is the gold ring on one officer's finger—
Marius's father, as it turns out. "[Thénardier] stooped down,
stayed crouched for a moment, and when he rose again there was
no ring on that hand," writes Hugo.[2]

This "corpse," he soon learns, is not dead; but that doesn't
deter the thief in the least. He tears off the man's Legion of Honor
cross, then pockets the man's purse and watch.

The officer opens his eyes and says something that surprises
the reader—and probably Thénardier, who must relish the man's
delusional state: "Thank you."[3]

The soldier believes the stranger bent over him has rescued
him when he has actually fleeced him. "Search my pockets," he
says, not realizing that has already been done. "You'll find a purse
there and a watch. Take them . . . You've saved my life."[4]

Colonel Georges Pontmercy, an officer of Napoléon's army, has been duped. And in so quickly thinking Thénardier is his savior, he brings to mind the subtle way we, too, give up our true riches to the things we unconsciously consider our saviors.

Work as savior, for example. How easily we live as if getting things done is that which sustains us. If I could live my life again—I'm fifty-nine as I write this—it is the thing I'd want to change most: the pace at which I've lived. I've raced from a day job (newspaper columnist) to freelance jobs (speaking, teaching, book writing). I take solace in the realization that I still managed to make nearly all my kids' baseball games, still stayed connected to my wife, and still found time for a quick vacation here and there. And yet it's been a life lived at far too fast a pace, the tyranny of the urgent becoming work, work, work. All robbing me of my time with those I love. Stealing too many would-be memorable moments that came and went without me noticing. Taking away too many opportunities to reach out to those in need. Pocketing my sense of peace—even as I whisper, "You've saved my life."

Achievement as savior. How easily we pay homage to accomplishing things as if they were saving us. We are slaves to the electronic to-do lists, all under the misguided notion that in achievement lies success. "We live in a highly competitive and individualistic society, and the pressures on us to strive, to achieve, to 'get ahead' are enormous," writes Paul Wachtel in *The Poverty of Affluence: A Psychological Portrait of the American Way of Life.* "There is a price to be paid—having continuously to face the question 'am I doing enough?' and, for many, never quite having the sense of one's work being done and it being time to relax . . . What we need now is not 'more.' What we need is a way off the treadmill."[5] And yet, even as we willingly pay this price—"You'll find a purse there and a watch"—so are we being robbed of the richer things. In Matthew 16:26, Jesus says, "What good will it be for someone to gain the whole world, yet forfeit their soul?"

Sometimes we don't even recognize who it is that's robbing us of that soul. What we need, then, is discernment to live for a higher purpose than the world's stress-for-success version. "Do not conform to the pattern of this world," says Romans 12:2, "but be transformed by the renewing of your mind. Then you will be able to test and approve what God's will is—his good, pleasing and perfect will."

That, of course, is no guarantee of a life without pain; consider Jean Valjean, who lets go of his anger and bitterness to begin anew yet still struggles through an array of obstacles. Nor is it a guarantee of public admiration; Thénardier's lies, after all, earn him glory and gratitude while Valjean's true heroism earns him persecution and jail time.

But at least the battles Valjean fights are for noble things worth fighting for and not for the things we think are sustaining us when they're actually stealing our souls.

Lesson 18

God's ways aren't always our ways

This man must be pardoned![1]

—THE CROWD, AFTER A CONVICT SAVES A SAILOR AT TOULON

AFTER COMING CLEAN BEFORE THE COURT THAT HE, MADELEINE, not the deranged man on the witness stand, is Jean Valjean, he flees but is captured a few days later and sent to the galleys in Toulon, on the coast of southern France.

In Toulon, the local newspaper later reports an amazing rescue. At port, a sailor working on high rigging grabs a rope to avoid a fall but winds up dangling like a stone at the end of a string. He is saved by a convict assigned to the ship. This is no small feat. The rescue is done with ropes high up on a mast of the ship and is watched by, writes Hugo, "ten thousand eyes" on shore.[2]

"The throng applauded; seasoned prison guards wept, women hugged each other on the wharves, and on all sides voices exclaimed, with emotion-shocked enthusiasm, 'This man must be pardoned!'"[3]

Then it happens. "Suddenly, terror ran through the crowd. Whether from fatigue or dizziness, the convict hesitated and staggered. All at once, the crowd shouted; the convict had fallen into the sea."[4]

The newspaper reports that, although no body has been found, the convict is presumed dead. "The man," says the story, "was registered under the number 9430, and his name was Jean Valjean."[5] The same Jean Valjean who later digs up a buried chest of his life's earnings near Montfermeil, where Cosette is living.

His supposed "death" in Toulon has brought him back to life, symbolic of how the life of faith can seem like a contradiction. In his willingness to die—to save the sailor—Jean Valjean essentially is resurrected. In his willingness to save another, Valjean goes from prisoner to free man.

Scripture is sprinkled with contradictions: The world suggests that the race is to the swift. But Matthew 19:30 says, "But many who are first will be last, and many who are last will be first." The world says the way up is up, but Scripture suggests the way up is down—on bended knee. "God opposes the proud but shows favor to the humble," says James 4:6. The world suggests that to receive, you go out and "get." But Acts 20:35 says, "It is more blessed to give than to receive."

One of the richest men I know lives in the poorest part of our town. He and his wife head up a grassroots ministry to the homeless, the thrust of which is handing out sandwiches and coffee to street people out of the back of their pickup truck. I've interviewed thousands of people in my career as a journalist, but he is among the most contented people I've ever known. He reminds us that God's ways are not man's way.

"For it is in giving that we receive," says the Prayer of Saint Francis of Assisi. "It is in pardoning that we are pardoned, and it is in dying that we are born to Eternal Life."

Lesson 19

NOT ALL THAT
GLITTERS IS GOLD

*A torn conscience leads to an unraveled life . . . [The Thénardiers]
belonged to that species of marauding sutlers we have described,
roaming the countryside, robbing here and selling there.[1]*

—LES MISÉRABLES

THE MUSICAL VERSION OF LES MISÉRABLES CLOAKS THE
Thénardiers in such comedic ambience that, at first glance, they
can come across as harmless misfits, fun-loving innkeepers who
lie, cheat, and steal while creating no-harm-no-foul debauchery.
And in a story that's often dark and depressing, you can appreciate
the need for some comic relief.

That said, Hugo does not let the couple off so easily. Though
the author's descriptions of them are, at times, humorous—"she
had the look of a market porter dressed in petticoats"[2]—he tints
them with a sense of vileness that other treatments of *Les Misérables*
do not, particularly old-time movie versions, some of which ignore
the couple completely.

Together, the husband and wife bring out the worst in each

other—and in others. "Their accord," writes Hugo, "had no other result than evil."[3]

There. He said it. The Thénardiers are evil. "Cosette," Hugo writes, "was beaten unmercifully; that came from the woman. She went barefoot in the winter; that came from the man. Cosette ran upstairs and downstairs; washed, brushed, scrubbed, swept, slaved away, breathless, lifted heavy things, and, puny as she was, did the hardest work."[4]

The couple pities her not, even as they continually harangue Fantine for more money to care for the little girl. "The Thénardier Tavern," writes Hugo, "was like a web in which Cosette had been caught and was trembling. The idea of oppression was realized in this dismal servitude. It was something like a fly serving spiders." They beat her, then say, "How ugly she is with her black eye."[5]

And yet, particularly when it came to guests, the Thénardiers are, as Hugo puts it, "clever." Simply put, their intent is to fleece everybody for as much as they can get, to, as he writes, "make the traveler pay for everything, including the flies his dog eats!"[6]

Hugo makes little mention of the guests' reaction to such, but the musical suggests that they are more than willing to do business with the Thénardiers—and, in some ways, happily ignorant of being fleeced.

Which raises the question: In twenty-first-century America, aren't many of us happily ignorant too?

I know; even raising the idea can be guilt-producing. You can't watch the innkeeper scenes from the 2012 movie version of *Les Misérables* without laughter, disgust, and pity for how stupid the customers are for being taken in by the conniving husband and wife. And yet, every day, isn't that exactly what Madison Avenue, advertising, television, and social media can do to us

—and subtly teach us to do to ourselves? Promise one thing (contentment) and deliver another (discontentment)? The subtle bait and switch? The "you can have it all" or "you deserve it" or "you better get this" lies?

Sure. We willingly let it welcome us in and become like the guests at the Thénardier Tavern. Wachtel writes:

> Our entire economic system is based on human desires being inexhaustible. Without always recognizing what we are doing, we have established a pattern in which we continually create discontent. This is not just something perpetrated by people in the advertising industry, though they are hardly innocent in it. And it is not the simple result of a deliberate conspiracy by the corporations, though they do indeed attempt to manipulate us to their advantage. Rather, it reflects a mentality we all share, something we all participate in.[7]

I remember a pastor writing about how content he felt one day as he mowed his lawn, utterly lacking nothing in his life. Then he cooled off with a lemonade and started thumbing through a magazine. He saw advertisements for riding lawn mowers—*Boy, wouldn't that be cool?* Features on swanky homes—*Goodness! Couldn't we use a three-car garage?* Notes about how a couple had upgraded their backyard—*Wouldn't a fountain be nice?* In a few short minutes he had gone from contentment to discontentment, from thinking he was a man without need to a man with all sorts of (expensive) needs, from satisfied to dissatisfied.

"In a Harlem tenement, or a village in India, one might well expect improvements in the material basis of life to be strongly associated with improvements in feelings of well-being," writes

Wachtel. But, he contends, in industrialized nations "the contribution of material goods to life satisfaction has reached a point of diminishing returns."[8]

Oh, the new car or jewelry or trip might temporarily bring a sense of well-being and peace, but it never lasts. Why? Because God wired us for relationships—with Him and with those around us. And we live in a world constantly cajoling us that contentment is found in changing our circumstances—e.g., buying new stuff, getting a shot of pleasure, upgrading to the latest version—until we quickly grow discontented, whereupon the cycle endlessly repeats.

Writes the apostle Paul in Philippians 4:11–13: "I have learned to be content whatever the circumstances. I know what it is to be in need, and I know what it is to have plenty. I have learned the secret of being content in any and every situation, whether well fed or hungry, whether living in plenty or in want. I can do all this through him who gives me strength."

On a short-term mission in Haiti, I was talking with an in-country missionary, an American who lived in the country full-time. "It must be hard leaving the comforts of the U.S. for the poverty of Haiti," I said.

I'll never forget her response.

"No," she said. "The hard part is going back to America, where people believe themselves to be so rich but, in a different way, are poorer and more desperate than the people here."

Lesson 20

GOD HEARS OUR DESPERATE CRIES FOR HELP

Oh my God! Oh God![1]

—COSETTE, WHILE SEEMINGLY ALONE IN THE WOODS

WHAT IS IT THAT ULTIMATELY BRINGS COSETTE TOGETHER WITH Jean Valjean? You could argue that it is Valjean's newfound freedom, his good fortune to survive a fall into the sea from a ship and manage to surface—perhaps an intentional "fall"—with the perfect opportunity to escape the life of a convict again. You could argue that it is the good fortune, as it turns out, of eight-year-old Cosette being sent to the woods at night to fetch water for the Thénardiers. But if each is a strand in the coming together of the two people, Hugo suggests that what actually twined them together is this: Cosette's crying out to God in her darkest hour—both literally and figuratively.

It is Christmas Eve 1823. At the Thénardier Tavern in Montfermeil, the horse of a newly arrived guest needs water, but the faucet has run dry. Never mind that the night is so dark one drinker says, "It is as black as an oven"[2]—the Thénardiers send the little girl away with a bucket nearly as large as she. She is petrified with fear. As long as she has a glint of light from the village, the little girl has at least a semblance of safety; "to go beyond the last booth had been difficult," writes Hugo. "To go further than the last house became impossible."[3]

As Cosette ventures into the woods, she is in an "impossible" situation. After drawing water from the spring, she sits down, racked with fear and fatigue. Then, writes Hugo, she looks up to a star. She starts home with the sloshing bucket of water. "At that moment," writes Hugo, "only the Eternal Father saw this sad thing." She rests at a chestnut tree, where the catalyst for change occurs. She cries out, "Oh my God! Oh God!"[4]

This from a little girl who, ostensibly, has never had anyone talk to her of this God, of this light in the darkness. But from this moment, nothing will be the same for her. "She suddenly felt that the weight of the bucket was gone. A hand, which seemed enormous to her, had just caught the handle."[5] She looks up as if a mirror of Psalm 121: "I lift up my eyes to the mountains—where does my help come from?" (v. 1).

And there is a stranger grasping the handle of her bucket—Jean Valjean.

If anything would send an afraid-of-the-dark little girl into shock, this would be it, wouldn't it? And yet, like the Christmas shepherds being encouraged by the angel to "fear not," the newcomer calms her. "The child," writes Hugo, "was not afraid."[6]

Valjean says of her bucket of water, "That's very heavy for you . . . Give it to me. I'll carry it for you."[7] It is Matthew 11:28–30 come to light in the forest darkness: "Come to me, all you who are weary and burdened, and I will give you rest. Take my yoke upon you and learn from me, for I am gentle and humble in heart, and you will find rest for your souls. For my yoke is easy and my burden is light."

"The man walked very fast," writes Hugo. "Cosette followed him without difficulty. She was no longer tired . . . She had never been taught to turn to Providence and pray. However, she felt in her heart something resembling hope and joy, which rose toward heaven."[8]

What's telling in this stranger who helps Cosette is not only what he does but what he does *not* do. Valjean does not scold her for being out in the woods alone, nor lecture her about the evils of the darkness, nor wag his finger with lessons. He instead eases her burden and begins learning *her* story. Asks her questions. Listens to find out just who she is. Buys her a doll.

At the Thénardier Tavern, he sees the cobweb-strewn nook beneath the stairs where Cosette is forced to sleep and drops a gold coin into one of her tattered shoes.

Finally, he sets her free by paying what amounts to a Thénardier-demanded ransom. As the two leave the next morning, writes Hugo, Cosette "walked along seriously, opening her large eyes and looking at the sky. She had put her coin in the pocket of her new apron. From time to time she bent over and glanced at it, and then looked at the man. She felt almost as though she were near God."[9]

Nearly two centuries later and in real life, the dark of night lingers. I think of homeless teenagers I once interviewed whose lives were full of such darkness, one of whom told me, "My dad died when I was eight of liver failure. Drinking. I raised myself. Nobody taught me anything but me." So she left home—at age nine.

She was a modern-day Cosette escaping a Thénardier world. The homeless that some people refer to as street rats. Black sheep. Throwaways. Druggies. Their only link to security is the basement of a church in our community, where volunteers provide warmth, clothing, and an occasional hot meal, bringing to life the "Come to me, all you who are weary and burdened" promise, "and I will give you rest."

Rich or poor, we're weighed down and made weary by burdens. But we can revel in this assurance: our cries in the darkness will not go unheard.

Lesson
21

CHILDREN NEED
CHILDHOODS

Play, my child.[1]

—JEAN VALJEAN, TO COSETTE

IN THE TAVERN RUN BY THE THÉNARDIERS WITH OVER-THE-top sweetness and underhanded schemes, Jean Valjean has come for Cosette. Fantine has given him signed permission to take her child, though, of course, the Thénardiers will not part with the girl without great bundles of cash. But when Valjean makes the first of many payments the Thénardiers will demand, it's telling what his first words are to Cosette.

"Play, my child," he says.

This is not a little girl used to the frivolity of childhood. Hers has been a life of duty, even though she is only eight. And so she is overwhelmed by this sudden freedom to "play." But when the Thénardiers' daughters, Éponine and Azelma, begin playing with a doll, Cosette's imagination goes to work. She dresses up a tiny lead sword in rags to pretend she, too, has a doll.

"A doll," Hugo reminds us, "is one of the most imperative

needs, and at the same time one of the most charming instincts of feminine childhood."[2]

When Valjean buys Cosette a doll she had been admiring in a nearby shop, he is giving her permission to use her imagination. She is transformed, as if, Hugo writes, "someone had said to her suddenly, 'Little girl, you are now Queen of France.'"[3]

Today some children, like Cosette under the thumbs of the Thénardiers, have been robbed of their childhoods. Poverty can do that. Parental addictions can do that. Physical or mental disabilities can do that. As a reporter and columnist, I've been in the homes of scores of children over the years who have been forced to bypass the joys of childhood.

Sad. But also sad are children who have little sense of play and imagination for the opposite reason: well-to-do parents who have so regimented their kids' lives with adult-supervised programs, with impossibly high standards, and with computer games requiring little imagination on the children's part. These kids, too, have been robbed of childhoods.

Hugo appreciates the wonders of childhood, even as he shows Cosette transitioning from essentially a slave to a little girl. But I wonder if parents today appreciate it enough. At the newspaper where I work, I was once responsible for a group of teenagers who wrote stories for one of our feature sections each week. I was amazed at how much pressure many of these kids—even as freshmen and sophomores—felt to get into the "right" college. I continue to be amazed at how orchestrated young people's lives are, leaving little time for kids to use their imaginations.

"One of the greatest phrases you can hear a child say is 'I'm bored,'" a teacher once told me. "Because when you allow children to come up with a solution for that boredom, that's when their imaginations go to work. It leads to another great phrase: 'Let's pretend.'"

Creativity among American children has declined in recent years, a 2010 study at the College of William and Mary found. Children are less able to produce unique and unusual ideas, less humorous, less imaginative, and less able to elaborate ideas. It's not that creativity can be lost; it's innate in children, researchers say. But it must be nurtured.[4]

Perhaps Hugo, in his work of fiction, gives Valjean better instincts than a man who has spent virtually no time around children deserved, but the new "parent" displays such nurturing in his first few hours with Cosette. He gives her permission to play and, with the doll, gives her the means to play.

We should do the same with our children, lest too many of them grow up without imagining that they are the queen of France or the supreme commander of some distant galaxy.

WE NEED ONE ANOTHER

When their two souls saw each other, they
recognized mutual need, and they embraced.[1]

—HUGO, ON VALJEAN AND COSETTE

AT FIRST GLANCE, COULD JEAN VALJEAN AND COSETTE BE ANY
more different? When they meet, he is a fifty-five-year-old man,
she an eight-year-old girl. He is a man of means and has been
mayor of a town and head of the town's most successful business. She is essentially a slave, an orphan, a Cinderella to the
Thénardiers' more valued two daughters.

And yet here's what the two have in common: both are lonely
souls.

Valjean has position, power, and affluence, but none can
replace the aching he has for human relationships. We're made to
love and to be loved. But until his new relationship with Cosette,
Valjean has not had any sustained relationships. Cosette, of
course, has experienced nothing but greed, cruelty, and insen-
sitivity from the Thénardiers. Given as much, it's surprising she
hasn't been warped by her experience; after all, we tend to become
that which we know.

Valjean's life of helping others might have given him a sense of satisfaction, but it certainly isn't enriching him in terms of relationships. The factory workers he employs live with a certain "at the end of the day" bitterness toward all around them. (Just as Valjean has before his conversion: "For I had come to hate the world," he sings in the musical, "this world that always hated me."[2]) Whenever he helps someone—the man under the cart, Fauchelevent, or Fantine when she is about to be sent to jail— he not only gets nothing in return but puts himself at risk. Each gesture deepens Javert's conviction that the man has, indeed, assumed a new identity. And with no visible connections to family, Valjean, like Cosette, is something of an orphan.

"Jean Valjean," writes Hugo, "had never loved anything. For twenty-five years he had been alone in the world. He had never been a father, lover, husband, or friend. In prison he had been cross, sullen, chaste, ignorant, and intractable . . . His sister and her children had left him only a vague distant memory, almost totally vanished. He had made every effort to find them again and, not succeeding, had forgotten them."[3]

Is Cosette so very different? She is so young when parting ways with her mother that she hardly remembers her. "Everybody had repelled her—the Thénardiers, their children, other children," writes Hugo. "She had loved the dog; it died and after that no one would have anything to do with her."[4]

But Cosette and Valjean each become the other's fulfillment, the missing piece in their life puzzles. "In that mysterious moment when their hands touched," writes Hugo, "they were welded together. When their two souls saw each other, they recognized mutual need, and they embraced."[5]

The bishop has brought one thing to Valjean's life; now Cosette has brought another. "The bishop," writes Hugo, "had caused the dawn of virtue on his horizon; Cosette invoked the dawn of love."[6]

After nearly four decades in the workplace, I've noticed a common denominator among people who esteem work above all else, who fight viciously over what you wouldn't think would be fall-on-the-sword issues, who come early, stay late, and work weekends. It's because this is all they have. Oh, they might be married, might even have children; but such people have been relegated to the background. In essence, workaholics are often lonely people for whom the office, not relationships, has become their be-all, end-all.

Javert is a perfect example. His work is his life. Hugo remains silent on the police inspector's background, but you get the idea he is not going home to the warmth of family. As Fantine is dying, this is a man so hardened against human relationships that his lone concern seems to be apprehending Jean Valjean. A man who, believing that Valjean did not drown in Toulon but might be alive and back in Montfermeil, interrogates the Thénardiers with virtually no concern about the wretched conditions Cosette has faced while living with the family.

"How sad," cowboy singer Dan Roberts says, "to love things that can't love us back." And how encouraging when people invest in one another.

"He loved, and he grew strong again," writes Hugo of Valjean with Cosette in his life. "Alas, he was as frail as Cosette. He protected her, and she gave him strength. Thanks to him, she could walk upright in life; thanks to her, he could persist in virtue. He was this child's support, and she his prop and staff. Oh, divine unfathomable mystery of Destiny's compensations."[7]

In short, as Valjean needs Cosette and she him, so do we need one another.

Lesson
23

FAITH MUST
TOUCH OTHERS

Morality is truth in full bloom.[1]
—*LES MISÉRABLES*

WITH JEAN VALJEAN AND COSETTE TAKING REFUGE FROM
Javert in a convent—he becomes a gardener, she a student—Hugo
uses the opportunity to expound on faith. It is a fascinating mean-
dering about life and God and the institutions that can suppress
the full expression of our faith, e.g., convents. But it begs a question that we dare not leave unanswered any longer: Spiritually,
where did Hugo stand?

It's complicated. Did he believe in God? Undoubtedly. But
Hugo never called himself a Christian nor was there much in his
life to suggest he was. "He was a deist of sorts," writes Addison
Hart in *Touchstone: A Journal of Mere Christianity*. (His poetry,
for example, indicates that he held to the concept of God that has
since been termed "panentheism," a belief that God both tran-
scends and permeates all creation.)[2]

And his personal life? Like us all, Hugo had his strengths and weaknesses. Unlike us all, he was revered by the people of France almost as if he were a god, having become, by 1851, the most famous writer in the world. And his vanity suggests he enjoyed it. "The truth is," writes G. K. Chesterton, "that Hugo represents all the ultimate and fundamental things—love, fury, pity, worship, hatred, and consequently, among other things, vanity."[3]

He had a longtime mistress, a relationship he began after learning of his wife's affair with his best friend. And if he possessed a generous spirit, cared deeply for the poor, and often expressed a certain affection for God's love, he was not a follower of Jesus in any practical sense.

What makes Hugo such an enigma is that *Les Misérables* brings the gospel to life with such utter clarity, passion, and precision. Hugo exemplifies the type of author once described by Thomas Merton:

> We have now become wise enough to realize that a writer can be profoundly biblical in his work without being a churchgoer or a conventional believer, and we are also aware of the fact that in our time it is often the isolated and lonely artist, facing the problems of life without the routine consolations of conventional religion, who really experience in their depth the existential dimension of those problems.[4]

Despite Hugo's distaste for the convent, he honors the pursuit of God in his description of Valjean living in it. ("A faith is a necessity to man. Woe to him who believes nothing."[5]) He champions the value of prayer. ("We bow to the man who kneels."[6]) He extols faith in action. ("Morality is truth in full bloom. Contemplation leads to action."[7])

To a man who believed the biblically sound concept that faith must become action, Hugo was no fan of the cloistered-convent life. Rather than give free expression to faith, he believed, it suffocated that faith. Rather than rejoice in God's love, it suppressed such love. ("These nuns are not joyous, rosy, and cheerful, as the daughters of the other orders often are. They are pale and serious."[8]) Rather than promote freedom of worship, it conscripted those within to a prison-like life of legalistic going-through-the-motions. Of the nuns he writes, "Their nerves have turned to bone, their bones to rock."[9]

Though his views belie a more modern version of convents, many of which involve themselves in loving outreach to the poor and sick, Hugo sees the nineteenth-century French convent as the manifestation of hypocrisy, the nuns turned inward in solemn exile, "their foreheads bowed but their souls so little uplifted."[10]

Sound familiar?

It's a reflection of some twenty-first-century churches in America. Full of people who ignore the call in Matthew 5:13–16 to be salt and light, but piously devote themselves to Sunday church, Bible study, and small groups. It's as if some have forgotten that these are the means to an end—ways to equip us to spread God's love—and not the ends in themselves. As if some have forgotten that though we are not *of* the world, we are to be *in* the world.

"Our Lord was not a recluse nor an ascetic," writes Oswald Chambers. "He did not cut himself off from society, but He was inwardly disconnected at all times."[11]

Jesus lived so much among the real world that some accused Him of being a glutton and wine bibber. But He knew then what we too often ignore now: there is no impact without contact.

"You are the light of the world," says Matthew. "A town built on a hill cannot be hidden. Neither do people light a lamp and put it under a bowl. Instead they put it on its stand, and it gives light to everyone in the house. In the same way, let your light shine before others, that they may see your good deeds and glorify your Father in heaven" (5:14–16).

At the end of each summer, churches in our community spread out to hundreds of schools to do work that the districts can't afford to do themselves. I'm guessing that those single days of action touch our community more deeply than all the Bible memorization that goes on within the city's borders if such lessons aren't put into practice. The fullness of our faith won't be found in sequestering ourselves off from the world in legalistic reverence, but rather in allowing such reverence to let our faith set sail to the wider world beyond.

Lesson 24

Don't rush to

judgment

*It is ourselves we have to fear. Prejudice is the
real robber, and vice the real murderer.*

—*Les Misérables*

Hugo is fairly harsh with his criticism of the nuns in
the convent, perhaps one of the reasons the Vatican banned the
book. And it may well reflect the reality of such places in nineteenth-century France. But if his assumption is that all nuns are
sour, inward-focused women who are spiritually suffocating from
legalistic constraints, such an assessment strikes of unwarranted
narrowness.

To assume we can paint an entire group of people with the
same brush is to take the easy way out instead of getting to know
people within a particular group. To believe in one-size-fits-all
thinking is to set yourself up to be a victim of the same assumption, should others do likewise about a group of which you're part.

"Do not judge, or you too will not be judged," says Matthew.

"For in the same way you judge others, you will be judged, and with the measure you use, it will be measured to you" (7:1–2).

Better to acknowledge that everyone—me, you, Hugo—has biases. And dare to see beyond them.

When a racial incident divided our community years ago, I didn't just pontificate about who was right and who was wrong; everyone was doing that. I enrolled in a community college multicultural class, which was enlightening and a tad guilt-producing because of the light it shined on some of what I realized were my own subtle biases.

I also found myself going back to a story I wrote for my high school paper about an exchange program that our nearly all-white high school had had with a predominantly black high school. I remember how many people from that high school charged that I had been unfair in my contrast. No way, I told myself at the time, and was reassured by an adviser and colleagues who agreed.

But with nearly four decades of insight, I reread that story. The students and faculty from the other school were right. My story had been unfair. The biases I couldn't see at the time had clouded my perspective. Acknowledging such doesn't preclude me from making that same mistake again, but it does heighten my awareness of how easily we can lump people together with one of those "If you're [fill in the blank] then-you must be [fill in the blank]" judgments.

Says James 2:1–4:

My brothers and sisters, believers in our glorious Lord Jesus Christ must not show favoritism. Suppose a man comes into your meeting wearing a gold ring and fine clothes, and a poor man in filthy old clothes also comes in. If you show special attention to the man wearing fine clothes and say, "Here's a good seat for you," but say to the poor man, "You stand there" or "Sit on the floor by my feet," have you not discriminated among yourselves and become judges with evil thoughts?

As I was reading *Les Misérables,* in particular the chapters about Hugo and his harsh criticism of the convent, I was also writing about a local nun for my newspaper column, a woman who was celebrating fifty years since taking her vows with the order that founded our community's largest hospital.

A member of the hospital's board referred to a quote from Mother Teresa in describing the honoree: "[She] once said, 'It is not how much we do, but how much love we put in the doing.' That's Sister Aileen."[1]

It was, said some, as if she saw people with CAT scan vision, beyond the obvious, to discover how they were hurting and how she could help. "She's the consummate listener," said the hospital's CEO. "Steadfast in prayer . . . steadfast in humor—and an occasional prank."

Sister Aileen had been known to tap-dance in the hallways, show up in a clown's suit, or distract an audience by swirling a laser pointer behind a speaker's head. And yet for all her humor, it was the serious way in which she valued others that shone brightest in her half century of service: Showing up in the middle of the night to comfort grieving families. Leading morning prayers at the hospital. Fighting for a neonatal unit back in the 1980s even though it looked as if it were a financial bridge too far.

"Because of her support then, and the support of the other sisters, the last three decades have seen thousands of babies saved who would otherwise have languished or been sent away," said the hospital's chief of medicine.

As I contrasted this with Hugo's harshness toward the nuns in the convent, it was a gentle reminder for me: don't lump individuals together and stamp your approval or disapproval on them. That may be easy but can lead to misjudgments and missing the human wonders among us.

Lesson 25

Faith in others unlocks their giftedness

Father Fauchelevent, I saved your life . . . Now
you can do for me what I once did for you.[1]

—Jean Valjean, to the convent gardener

Jean Valjean and Cosette find refuge in the convent of
Petit-Picpus in Paris. There Valjean meets a gardener, Fauchelevent,
whose life he once saved in Montreuil-sur-Mer when the man was
pinned beneath a cart.

When the accident occurred, Fauchelevent had fallen on hard
times and was jealous of Madeleine's rise to prominence as mayor
and as a factory owner. After the cart incident, Madeleine arranges
for him to get work as a gardener at the convent.

But, in vintage-Hugo fashion, it isn't until 290 pages later when
the author connects this foreshadowed loop. On a moonlit night,
Valjean and Cosette—with Inspector Javert in pursuit—enter a
convent where, if the fugitive does not recognize the gardener, the
gardener certainly recognizes him.

"I'm the one you got the position for here," says Fauchelevent. "You saved my life."[2]

It is a meager life at best, we soon learn. Fauchelevent is a beaten-down man. "Something resembling a man was walking among the glass bells in the melon patch," writes Hugo, "rising up, bending over, stopping, with a regular motion. This being seemed to limp."[3]

To warn them of Fauchelevent's presence, the nuns have required him to wear a bell strapped to his leg as if, writes Hugo, he were "a ram or a cow." Every ring of that bell reminds Fauchelevent that he is to be avoided. His life, it seems, has little meaning; he works the garden, lives in a "lone shanty,"[4] and literally stays out of people's way. That's it: the totality of his purpose. That is, until two years later, when along comes Jean Valjean.

The newcomers change everything. Valjean trusts in Fauchelevent to orchestrate an elaborate scheme that would secure him a job as an "assistant gardener," duping the nuns into believing he is the man's brother. Meanwhile, in a bizarre plot involving Valjean being placed in a coffin, Fauchelevent manages the delicate task of assisting the Reverend Mother regarding the final wishes of a recently deceased nun—and legitimizing Valjean as worthy to stay on at the convent.

Why does his life go from meaningless to meaningful? Because someone—Jean Valjean and, to a lesser degree, the Reverend Mother—believes in him. And great things can happen when, at first, we believe the best in those around us.

Fauchelevent is the nineteenth-century French version of "Shooter" Flatch (Dennis Hopper), the town drunk and father of one of Hickory High's players in the 1986 movie *Hoosiers*. He is a former-basketball-star-turned-alcoholic whom Coach Norman

Dale (Gene Hackman) allows—against the will of some fans—to be an assistant coach, in part because Dale admires his basketball knowledge and in part to help him escape the bottle.

Coach Dale goes so far as to have himself kicked out of a game, just to give Shooter a chance to lead. And if Shooter initially freezes up as if struck by a stun gun, he soon rises to the occasion, setting up the winning play with only seconds left in the game.

Why did this all happen? Because one man believed in someone whom most people did not.

"Let us consider how we may spur one another on toward love and good deeds," says Hebrews 10, "not giving up meeting together, as some are in the habit of doing, but encouraging one another" (vv. 24–25).

Everyone has God-given gifts that can make the world a better place. But it's up to us to help unlock those gifts. To believe in people in ways that we haven't in the past. And to help them find a deeper sense of purpose in the process.

THE PAST CAN BE
A SPRINGBOARD TO
THE FUTURE

Anyone who has been a prisoner knows the art of making himself small to match the diameter of the escape hatch.[1]

—HUGO, IN REFERENCE TO JEAN VALJEAN'S IDEA OF
BEING SLIPPED OUT OF THE CONVENT IN A COFFIN

FAUCHELEVENT IS INCREDULOUS AT JEAN VALJEAN'S IDEA TO hide in a coffin so he can get out of the convent and return as the gardener's "brother." But such a plan is almost second nature to Valjean, who has escaped from prison on numerous occasions.

Writes Hugo, "To be nailed up and carried out in a chest like a bundle, to live a long time in a box, to find air where there is none, to hoard his breath for hours at a time, to know how to be stifled without dying—that was one of Jean Valjean's saddest talents."[2]

The success of his plan demonstrates how the past can empower our future. The idea isn't to dwell on the darkness of our pasts; the apostle Paul, in Philippians 3:13, talks about "forgetting what is behind and straining toward what is ahead." But Scripture is full of stories about those who are empowered by remembering where they once were and how far they've come; Paul's appreciation of his new life in Christ only comes when he contrasts it against the old. In the Old Testament, people honor God by building memorial altars marking His faithfulness—faithfulness that could only be measured by looking at how far along He'd brought them compared to where they had been.

Consider Jean Valjean's early years in Montreuil-sur-Mer. His goodness overflows because of the badness of his past. Hugo writes that whenever Mayor Madeleine would hear of a down-and-outer looking for chimneys to sweep, "the mayor would send for him, ask his name, and give him money."[3] Why? Because of his last truly evil act: taking money from the young chimney sweep, Petit Gervais. His remembrance of his past empowers his present.

His goodness overflows because he never forgets the words of the bishop, whose admonition in the musical is for Valjean to "use this precious silver to become an honest man."[4]

In Annie Dillard's book *The Writing Life,* a photographer enters the same picture each year in a contest. It never wins an award. "You submit this same landscape every year, and every year I put it on the bad stack," a judge finally says. "Why do you like it so much?" The young photographer says, "Because I had to climb a mountain to get it."[5]

I can relate. One of the reasons my wife, Sally, and I have a marriage closing in on forty years is that, beyond her patience with my obsessive work habits, we've never forgotten how hard we fought to be together in the first place. We met the summer before I left to go away to college; she still had a year of high school left. And there came a point where we had to answer the question, was this just a summer fling, or were we in this for the long haul? Four decades, two children, and five grandchildren later, the answer is clear. But we never forget the three years we spent apart as we struggled to grow our early relationship.

We wrote letters nearly daily. Never dated anyone else. And withstood the pain of short visits followed by long good-byes. All to enable us to be together for a lifetime. Short-term pain for long-term gain.

Like all marriages, ours isn't perfect. But if we have a falling-out, I always remind myself how we struggled to preserve what we had. How desperately we longed to be together once and for all. And that perspective helps me overcome whatever challenge we're facing.

In other words, what adds to our appreciation of our marriage is the idea that we "had to climb a mountain to get it."

The past can be a springboard to our futures. That doesn't mean we stay tethered to that past, as slaves to, say, an unhappy childhood or other painful experiences. It *does* mean that acknowledging where we've been can help us get to where we need to go. "I have learned now," writes C. S. Lewis, "that while those who speak about one's miseries usually hurt, those who keep silent hurt more."

Remembering empowers us. Some people let the past strap them down like tethers on a hot-air balloon. Jean Valjean uses it to help him fly higher than anyone might have dreamed. Think about it: whenever he moves, he takes something with him: the candlesticks, symbols of his shame and evilness, yes, but also a reminder of who he no longer is—and why.

Lesson
27

Paying it forward
changes the world

It's my turn now.[1]

—Fauchelevent, regarding Valjean
having once saved him

When Fauchelevent meets Jean Valjean at the convent and realizes he is a man in need, he doesn't hesitate to help. Why? Because he has been helped himself—by this very man. The man who had lifted the horse cart that had pinned him to the ground.

"Fauchelevent was groping among conjectures," writes Hugo, "but saw nothing clearly except this: Monsieur Madeleine has saved my life. This single certainty was enough, and convinced him. He said to himself: 'It's my turn now.'"[2]

In doing so, he symbolically reflects 1 John 4:19: "We love because he first loved us."

The idea isn't to create eye-for-an-eye obligation for good. It isn't to keep track of who has given to you so you can make sure to pay that person back with exact change. It isn't to create some legalistic system that requires us to never owe anyone anything.

The idea instead is to understand that grace shown to us should become grace we show to others. That we can thank God for His sacrifices in how we live out our daily lives by doing so. That we don't so much pay *back* love, but pay *forward* love.

Recently, I was headed to an NCAA regional baseball game when someone gave me four nice tickets. I already had tickets. So I took the four and, before the game, offered them to people standing in the ticket line. They all responded the same way: At first, slightly suspicious that I was giving away great seats worth twenty dollars each. Then, assured that this was no con job, thankful that I'd made the offer. And finally, insistent that I be compensated.

"But why should I be paid for something I didn't have to pay for myself?" I said to one man. "The tickets were a gift to me. I'm just making them a gift to you."

He stood there, oddly uncomfortable with what he saw as an imbalance of goodness.

"The price you pay," I joked, "is having to sit next to me."

He laughed. "Well, at least let me buy you a hot dog."

"No need for that," I said, "but someday pay forward the kindness to someone else."

Years ago, a reader of the newspaper column I write came to me with a request. "I make good money. I want to see that some of it gets in the hands of people in need. I'm tired of just writing checks for nonprofits. And I wonder if you might dispense it at street level. You know; do some random acts of kindness on my behalf."

He then peeled off ten one-hundred-dollar bills.

Thus began a tradition at Christmastime. He gives me the money. I dispense it to people in need, buying groceries for a down-and-out mother and father in a small town, helping out a child-care center that is a month behind on a utility payment, even standing on a street corner with a cardboard sign that says, "Free $10 bills." (Talk about people being suspicious! I couldn't *give* that money away—literally.)

But one of the more memorable gifts was a one-hundred-dollar bill I gave to a guy who delivered potato chips to local stores, a guy, I figured, who could use a little extra cash at Christmas. "I'm spreading holiday cheer on behalf of an anonymous 'elf,' and was led to give you this," I said.

He took the money with all the enthusiasm of a tollbooth collector and started talking to me about something else, basketball, I believe. *Huh?* While I wasn't giving away the money for the purpose of getting wild responses in return, I walked to my truck thinking, *That was odd.*

For days, his response—or lack thereof—nagged at me. Then I got a phone call. It was him. "I'm sorry if I didn't seem more appreciative of the gift," he said. "I *was*. But I was just so stunned. And, well, I felt kind of guilty. I'm gettin' by. Doin' okay. But I have this neighbor who has been through two brain surgeries this year and doesn't have much money. I was wondering: Would it be okay if I gave the money to her?"

"Of course," I said.

Back in the store it had been my turn to bless. Now it was his turn. That's how it works. God blesses us. We bless others. And in a perfect world, the blessings roll forward like ripples on the water.

We can hoard all the pebbles we want, but they mean little until we toss them in the water.

A CONTENTED LIFE IS A THANKFUL LIFE

*His whole heart melted in gratitude
and he loved more and more.*[1]

—HUGO, ON VALJEAN

IMAGINE YOURSELF AS JEAN VALJEAN LIVING IN THE CONVENT with Cosette. You once were the highly esteemed mayor of a town that looked upon you as something of its savior. Little children followed you around the village with glee. Adults nodded and smiled their respect. Servants fetched whatever you wanted. Factory workers obeyed your commands. Citizens, for the most part, followed the rules you oversaw.

Now you are a gardener in a convent. Not even the chief gardener. An assistant to a man of little respect, Fauchelevent. You have little freedom. Your life is confined to a courtyard walled off from the rest of the world. You are enclosed in what Hugo describes as a prison of a different kind. You eat the same food every day. Walk the same ground. Sleep in the same bed in a shed probably the size of a college dorm room. Speaking of which, you have a roommate who is old, frail, and though he likes you now—you saved his life—he detested you when you were mayor of Montreuil-sur-Mer. So you could still be bitter about that.

And there's more. You must live under an assumed identity. Your name is Jean Valjean, though when you entered here, you had been living under the assumed name of Monsieur Madeleine. You introduced yourself at the convent as "Ultimus," but the nuns call you "the other Fauvent," the last stop on the humility bus line before "Hey, you." So you've gone from "Monsieur Mayor" to "the other Fauvent."

You must live with the fear that Javert lurks outside to arrest you and send you back to prison, which would mean separation from the person you love more than anyone or anything in the world, Cosette. Thus, when there is an errand to run outside the convent, Fauchelevent, not you, gets a glimmer of life outside the walls.

Cosette is your life. You once spent day after day with her, but now that she is in school, you are allowed only one hour a day with her.

There; that is your new life. Now, could you imagine yourself in such conditions living as a thankful person?

Valjean does. "Within [these walls] he could see enough of the sky to be serene, and enough of Cosette to be happy," writes Hugo. "A very pleasant life began again for him."[2] He prays with deep gratitude each day at dusk. He thinks about how the convent is filling a life need—a humbling of sorts, putting a stop to what might have been a slipping back to the bitterness of a convict or the virtuous pride of a mayor. He sees the walls not as lions threatening him but as "encircling lambs."[3]

"His whole heart melted in gratitude," writes Hugo, "and he loved more and more."[4]

In recent years, I've read—and reread—an insightful book, *One Thousand Gifts: A Dare to Live Fully Right Where You Are* by Ann Voskamp, in which she expands on the same thankfulness Valjean does. Not as someone trapped in a convent, but as a self-described farmer's wife and mother of six children, whom she has homeschooled. "I feel just a tad bit overwhelmed and crazy," she writes.[5]

But she's a thankful woman. She challenges readers to literally count their blessings—I'm on number 288, "home sweet home"—and writes about living thankfully with grace, wisdom, truth, and more than a little literary panache. She is not reinventing the wheel here, but does a better job of inspiring everyday thankfulness than anyone I've read. "Our fall," writes Voskamp, "is always first a failure to give thanks."[6] It is all about perspective. Recognizing that our contentedness begins with thankfulness—and thus does she see, not oppression in a sink full of dishwashing soap bubbles, but wonder in the way the sunlight and soap create a rainbow of colors.

It begins, she says, with our attitudes toward God. Not one of smug expectations—"for although they knew God," says Romans 1:21, "they neither glorified him as God nor gave thanks to him"—but one of daily thankfulness.

As with Valjean at the convent, we are bound not by our circumstances, our physical surroundings, and our challenges, but instead by where our hearts lie and how our eyes see. It's our choice: bitterness or thankfulness?

WISDOM CAN COME FROM WEIRD PLACES

God has his own ways.[1]

—*LES MISÉRABLES*

DESPITE HUGO'S OBVIOUS DISLIKE OF CONVENTS, HE CREDITS one as putting an important piece in the puzzle that is becoming Jean Valjean: "The convent contributed, like Cosette, to confirm and complete in Jean Valjean the bishop's work," he writes.[2]

That's high praise. The bishop, of course, is the one whose mercy has set Valjean free to become a new man. And yet Valjean's time as a gardener in the convent also proves to be a fruitful experience while he avoids the snares of Javert. The experience nurtures him with a sense of humility.

The setting keeps his focus on the grace of the bishop instead of on the greed of the men whose "robbery, fraud, violence, lust, homicide" had led them to be his prison mates on the slave galleys.[3]

"So long as he compared himself only with the bishop, he had found himself unworthy and remained humble," writes Hugo, "but, for some time now, he had been comparing himself with the rest of men, and pride was springing up in him. Who knows? He might have finished by going gradually back to hatred. The convent stopped him in his descent."[4]

In the book, Hugo allows Valjean a broader mind about convents than he, as an author, expresses. He contrasts what he refers to as Valjean's two "prisons"—the actual one in Toulon and the virtual one in Paris. "Two seats of slavery," he writes.[5] And yet, in the women's devotion to prayer, in their innocence, in their regiment aimed at purity, Valjean sees a certain virtue in the convent that he had not found in prison.

"In the first, the captives were chained by chains alone; in the other, chained by faith." The first produces "desperate depravity, a cry of rage against human society, sarcasm against heaven." The second? "Benediction and love." In the evenings, he kneels in prayer before the sister performing the reparation. "It was as though he did not dare kneel directly before God."[6]

Valjean realizes he has learned from both experiences, honing a sense of humility toward self and reverence for God. "Had it not been for the [prison], he would have fallen back into crime," writes Hugo, "and had it not been for the [convent], into punishment."[7]

All of which serves as a reminder that God can teach us through the most unlikely experiences, people, and places: through injustice (in Valjean's case, a prison where he is sent for stealing a loaf of bread), through inconvenience (certainly life in the convent provides a few), even through exile (life among the nuns to avoid Javert's detection).

In 1945, Aleksandr Solzhenitsyn, the Russian writer and dissident, was arrested and exiled, ultimately to a number of Russian prisons and work camps. During an eleven-year imprisonment, he developed cancer. But amid such darkness he found light; amid hopelessness, hope; amid godlessness, God. He went on to write such classics as *One Day in the Life of Ivan Denisovich*. He won a Nobel Prize. He trumpeted the idea of individual responsibility, the idea that the world is not divided into good guys and bad guys. "The line dividing good and evil," he writes, "cuts through the heart of every human being."[8]

He spent more than fifty years studying the Russian Revolution and the disaster that followed.

> I have read hundreds of books, collected hundreds of personal testimonies, and have already contributed eight volumes of my own toward the effort of clearing away the rubble left by that upheaval. But if I were asked today to formulate as concisely as possible the main cause of the ruinous revolution that swallowed up some 60 million of our people, I could not put it more accurately than to repeat: "Men have forgotten God; that's why all this has happened."[9]

It is uncanny that a man could spend more than a decade in cancer-stricken captivity and come out with vision so pure. Or is it uncanny that people can live in total freedom, bathed in luxury and comfort—and *not*?

At any rate, God sends us life lessons on pleasant breezes and on ill winds. It's up to us to raise our sails and, like Jean Valjean, let them take us where we need to go.

TRUE CHARACTER IS
CONSISTENT CHARACTER

There are many great deeds done in the small struggles of life.[1]
—*LES MISÉRABLES*

WHAT DISTINGUISHES JEAN VALJEAN ISN'T ONLY THE DECI-
sions he makes with others in mind. It's that he does so over and
over—and not with the intent to impress anyone, because most
of his acts are done in total obscurity. If you're looking for a true
mark of character, that's it: Not just integrity exemplified here
and there. But integrity exemplified time and again throughout
the passing years, despite changing circumstances. And integrity
whether anyone happens to be watching.

"The test of a man's religious life and character is not what he
does in the exceptional moments of life, but what he does in the
ordinary times," writes Oswald Chambers.[2]

Sure, Valjean has his moments of public grandeur: Saving
Fauchelevent from death as people watch him lift the cart from
the man. Bursting into the courtroom to spare Champmathieu
from injustice as onlookers gasp. Rescuing the sailor on the ship

in front of, writes Hugo, "ten thousand eyes."[3] But what makes his life remarkable is the difference he makes in obscurity, the exclamation point of which is his journey through the sewer with Marius on his back.

We live in a world of one-hit wonders—as did Hugo, the author. "Win in the lottery," he writes, "and you are an able man."[4] Today, people can gain instant notoriety for one great athletic season or World Series or even one game, one great political move, one great song, one great splash upon the stage of whatever reality show happens to be hot.

But that moment doesn't define who that person is. Too often, the moment of glory is an aberration, a right-place-at-the-right-time opportunity that fades fast, leaving the person with a false sense of self-worth and leaving his or her publisher with a warehouse full of unbought books.

In *Les Misérables,* I think of the Thénardiers who, to benefit themselves, change their personas based on the circumstances; they become chameleons whose stock and trade is deception. Or these days, of politicians who will shift positions on issues to gain votes. Of people whose Facebook posts paint them with a nobility their offline lives might not support. Or of the pastor of a huge church I briefly attended: charismatic, handsome, well-read, passionate, and polished in the pulpit. Within a few years of us moving on to another church, however, he was but a shell of his former self—or, more accurately, his true self had been exposed, revealing a hypocritical man who'd been cheating on his wife. He lost it all: his family, his church, his respect, having been unmasked as a religious Wizard of Oz: all style, no substance.

Was that man redeemable and deserving of a second chance? Certainly. When we stop believing in grace and mercy for all, we start believing in a scorekeeper God whose highest expectation for us is a plethora of "works" and not a heart sold out to Him. But even such mercy can't erase the consequences of wrong living.

I think back to how impressive the minister could be in front of an audience and admit that I was duped; I'd totally bought into this guy as some sort of spiritual gold standard. But what you see isn't always what you get. What someone is like in the spotlight is not always what he or she is like in the shadows.

"We are not made for the mountains, for sunrises, or for the other beautiful attractions in life," writes Oswald Chambers. "Those are simply intended to be moments of inspiration. We are made for the valley and the ordinary things of life, and that is where we have to prove our stamina and strength."[5] He writes of life not being about "mounting up with wings," but about "walking and not fainting."[6]

My wife's grandmother was someone who understood this. A simple farm woman whose life was indelibly woven with character. Looking back, I realize she was simply a more agrarian version of Bishop Myriel. I entered her life at age nineteen, a long-haired, overall-wearing kid whose faith was young and untested—and who was dating her granddaughter. She accepted me on the spot. And in the twenty-five years I knew her, she never wavered in her unconditional love for me, for her family, and for essentially anyone she met. In *Where Roots Grow Deep* I wrote of her:

> She made a conscious decision to live a godly life, but I am not sure she understood how much we all noticed. In the seemingly pedantic ways of life, she offered the profound, and made of the commonplace something inspiring . . . She wasted nothing, including time. Or the chance to make a child happy.

If grandkids wanted to walk in mud puddles she would slap plastic bags over their shoes and let 'em wade . . . She didn't preach God's love; she lived it.[7]

She was made of the same stuff that Valjean and the bishop are, something to which we should aspire: a consistency of character that stands the test of time.

Lesson 31

REMEMBER THE HUMANITY OF THE HOMELESS

His father never thought of him, and his mother did not love him.[1]

—HUGO, ON GAVROCHE

HUGO PAINTS GAVROCHE, A LITTLE HOMELESS BOY, AS A FREE-spirited wanderer of the Paris streets, a "roguish urchin who looked both lively and sickly. He would come and go, sing, play pitch and toss, scrape the gutters, steal a little, but he did it cheerfully like the cats and the sparrows, laughed when people called him a brat, and got angry when they called him a guttersnipe."[2]

Above all, Hugo reminds us that Garroche is human, that he is not unlike better-off people except he has taken to the streets because he is not wanted elsewhere. His parents are the innkeepers who have "taken care" of Cosette, the Thénardiers. "But his father never thought of him, and his mother did not love him," writes Hugo. "He was one of those children so deserving of pity above all others, who have fathers and mothers and yet are orphans."[3]

How easy it is to look at the homeless and forget their

humanity; to forget that each came crying into this world like us. That each was created by the same God as us. That each, when young, harbored dreams like us.

I've spent enough time interviewing the homeless to understand that they are far more like "the rest of us" than "the rest of us" might presume. Yes, the streets are sprinkled with those suffering from mental problems, from addictions, from abuse. Some have made poor choices, hurt others, and hid from the law. But most are there, I'm convinced, for the same reason Gavroche is there: because at one point in their lives they felt more at home on the streets than they did at home.

"This little boy," Hugo writes, "never felt so happy as when in the street. For him the pavement was not so hard as the heart of his mother. His parents had kicked him out into life. He had simply taken flight."[4]

I once interviewed a sixteen-year-old girl, Angel, who told me she'd been homeless since age nine. She said her mother was a stripper, her father a bartender. At times, she lived with her mom in a van, at times with her father in other people's houses. "I left because I knew I could do better on my own," she said.

Most of the young homeless are on the streets because it beats the dysfunctional homes where they aren't loved. "Maybe one in fifty of these kids comes from a good, solid family," the director of a church-based homeless hub for teenagers told me.

Like Gavroche, many make the most of their homelessness. "Poverty," writes Hugo, "is like everything else. It gradually becomes endurable." Many rationalize that this is where they want to be. Many are straight from Hugo's line about Gavroche: "He had no shelter, no food, no fire, no love, but he was lighthearted because he was free."[5]

Hugo was a wealthy man. And yet he always had a heart for the homeless, the down-and-outers, *les misérables*—"the miserable ones." (A modern translation, writes Hugo biographer Graham Robb, might be "scum of the earth" or "the wretched.") "Written for the masses, Hugo's novel placed itself at the side of the individual," writes Robb. "It was history from the point of view of the scapegoat."[6]

Scapegoats who, when given a chance, can rise to so much more. One of the more inspiring subjects I've been privileged to write about was a man from Central America who, because of abject poverty, lived much of his childhood in a large cardboard box; he is now a successful business owner, community contributor, husband, and father.

Writes Hugo, "These bare feet, these naked arms, their rags, these shades of ignorance, depths of despair, the gloom can be used for the conquest of the ideal. Look through the medium of the people, and you will discern the truth. This lowly sand that you trample underfoot, if you throw it into the furnace and let it melt and seethe, will become sparkling crystal."[7]

But only if we see beyond such people's poverty and into their humanity.

Lesson
32

REMEMBER THOSE
WHO PUT THEIR
LIVES ON THE LINE

Monsieur Prosecutor, am I allowed to wear my scar?[1]
—GEORGES PONTMERCY, TO THE KING'S PROSECUTOR

BEFORE WE LEARN MUCH ABOUT MARIUS, THE YOUNG MAN who falls in love with Cosette—and a character Hugo created after himself as a young man—we learn about Marius's father. He's already mentioned in the book: George Pontmercy is the soldier at Waterloo in 1815 from whom Thénardier steals but who, thinking the swindler has saved his life, thanks the thief profusely and vows never to forget him.

Even if deluded in his injury-induced state, Pontmercy is a heroic soldier. "At Waterloo," writes Hugo, "it was he who took the colors from the Lunenburg battalion. He carried the colors to the emperor's feet. He was covered with blood from a saber stroke across his face received while seizing the banner."[2]

However, after the war he is all but forgotten. "The king, Louis

XVIII, ignoring all that had been done in the Hundred Days, recognized neither his position as officer of the Legion of Honor, nor his rank of colonel, nor his title of baron." In fact, after Pontmercy appears in public while wearing his rosette of an officer of the Legion of Honor, the king's prosecutor "notified him that he would be prosecuted for 'illegally' wearing this decoration."[3]

His reply: "I do not know whether it is that I no longer understand French, or that you no longer speak it; but the fact is I do not understand you." He continues to wear the rosette. Shortly thereafter, he again sees the prosecutor and asks, "Am I allowed to wear my scar?"[4]

I understand his pain. Not because I was once a soldier but because I've written about so many soldiers who know this pain. How can I forget Don Malarkey, one of the "Band of Brothers" whom I wrote about in the World War II book *Easy Company Soldier*, telling me how, decades after the war was over, he would go to a bar each night on his way home from work? "In the bottom of my glass of scotch," he said, "I could see the faces of every man we left in Bastogne."[5]

Nothing is sadder than a soldier forgotten, nothing more uplifting than a soldier remembered. In the spring of 2012, I had the privilege of accompanying an Honor Flight contingent to Washington, DC—World War II veterans given all-expense-paid trips to see the memorials that recognize their sacrifices but that they had never seen. Now, nearing the end of their lives, they were getting that chance.

They found those monuments meaningful. But what they found even more meaningful were the responses from people along the journey: At Portland (Oregon) International Airport, as the men walked—and some rolled in their wheelchairs—down the concourse, the patrons of a restaurant rose as one to give them a standing ovation. In Washington, DC, firefighters shot an arc of water over their plane in a salute of the men's service. On the last night before our return, the men gathered in the hotel lobby for "mail call"; each received a handful of letters from friends and family thanking him for his sacrifices. One of the more stoic guys melted into tears.

They'd hoped their sons and daughters wouldn't have to go to war; alas, Korea, Vietnam, the Persian Gulf, Iraq, and Afghanistan followed. Wars that weren't as black and white as World War II. But, like all wars, they took their tolls—and left thousands wearing "the scar," as does Pontmercy.

On Memorial Day 2013, I spoke at an event where an eighty-eight-year-old Pearl Harbor survivor, Bill Kunkle, shuffled to the front seat in the chapel. The event's director whispered to him, "Mr. Kunkle, at the end of the service, we'd like to honor you with the ceremonial flag." Kunkle wondered if there had been some mistake, he said later. A guy who'd been sent home from Hawaii by the navy because he'd been so emotionally racked by war?

Kunkle's eyes glistened. His head nodded slightly. As promised, honor guards unfolded and refolded the American flag, then presented it to Kunkle. He took it and held it to his chest as a mother might hold a newborn.

"It was one of the greatest days of my life," Kunkle later told me after I wrote about the incident in the *Register-Guard*. "I am so grateful."

As we all should be for people like him.

Lesson
33

Deceit is no respecter
of social standing

*The child would have been the colonel's joy in his solitude, but
the grandfather had imperiously demanded his grandson . . .[1]*

—Hugo, on Marius

Marius's father, the disrespected soldier, has
virtually no part in his son's life, though not by choice. In 1815,
the same year Jean Valjean escapes from prison, Pontmercy's
wife dies, leaving a child, Marius. The boy's maternal grandfather, Gillenormand, demands that the boy become his to raise.
Gillenormand is a staunch supporter of the monarchy and a
highly esteemed part of the Paris bourgeois. He is at political
odds with his son-in-law Pontmercy, who, writes Hugo, "refused
royal authority."[2]

Gillenormand lets the political differences between the
two carve a canyon through their relationship. He more than
demands custody of Marius; he threatens to disinherit the boy
if he is not turned over to him and his sister. Pontmercy loves
his son. But, writes Hugo, he "yielded for the sake of the little

boy."[3] And turns further inward, into a quiet life of gardening and going to Mass.

Against such selfless love we have Gillenormand, the societal opposite to "*les misérables*." Highbrow. Esteemed. Loyal to the Crown. And yet, despicable in the sense that he would, to soothe his political ego, separate a son from his father and convince the young man that his father is dishonorable. A father, mind you, whom Gillenormand's daughter chose to marry.

The point? Deceit is more easily recognizable in prison overalls, in the uniform of an enemy soldier, in the tattered garb of a guy pushing a stolen grocery cart. But it hides well amid esteem and money and position. It blends in well with the surroundings, churches included.

So it is that Gillenormand not only takes the boy but proceeds, over the years, to undermine the father in front of his son. He allows no communication between the two, mocks the man's noble war experience, and gets the very results he sought: "[Marius] came little by little to think of his father only with shame and with a closed heart." His father loves Marius deeply; a priest, at Mass, notices the man with "the scar on his cheek, and the tears in his eyes." The father writes Marius "tender letters, which the grandfather shoved into his pocket without reading."[4] Not hearing from the man, Marius is convinced his father does not love him.

For all the pomp and circumstance of his monied life, Gillenormand is no different from someone else who plunders Pontmercy more overtly: Thénardier, who steals the man's possessions—essentially, all that the man has—while the soldier lies wounded on the battlefield. Now, years later, Gillenormand steals all that Pontmercy has: His son. His respect. His honor.

Duplicity hides well in the fineries of wealth and the pulsing of power. Consider the modern-day "ministers of God" who preach the name-it-and-claim-it prosperity gospel, live in multimillion-dollar homes, and justify their zeal for materialism by twisting Scripture. To preach "It's God's will for you to live in prosperity instead of poverty" is like Gillenormand hiding the truth—the letters—from Marius. In doing so, that's hiding God's truth from a congregation. "Be on your guard against all kinds of greed," says Jesus in Luke 12:15. "Life does not consist in an abundance of possessions."

Again and again, Scripture is clear that God values humility and the heart. And we're wise to be swayed by such, not by those who use their lofty positions to deceive.

Lesson 34

THE TRUTH SHALL
SET YOU FREE

*Well! Poor child, you can say you had a
father who loved you dearly.*[1]

—A PRIEST, TO MARIUS, AFTER THE
YOUNG MAN'S FATHER HAS DIED

MARIUS IS NOW A YOUNG MAN. WHEN HIS FATHER DIES, HE feels nothing, even if he has enough ego that he doesn't want others to suspect he feels nothing. When he arrives at his father's deathbed, a servant, a priest, and a doctor are misty-eyed at the passing of Georges Pontmercy. Obviously, the man has touched lives, but not his son's. "Marius, too little moved, felt ashamed and embarrassed by his attitude," writes Hugo. "He had his hat in his hand, he let it drop to the floor to make them believe that grief left him without the strength to hold it."[2]

Though he feels badly about his attitude, Marius justifies it. "He did not love his father, and that was all there was to it," writes Hugo.[3]

But two things happen that change how he sees his father.

First, a priest who'd known his father—while not even realizing Marius is the man's son—honors Georges Pontmercy with a story about the faithfulness of a particular father: how the man, for ten years, would regularly come to Mass and hide behind a pillar, just to see his estranged son.

"The little one never suspected that his father was here," says the priest to Marius. "Perhaps he did not even know that he had a father." But he did, the priest says. And he was a "poor, brave father" who would see his son at Mass and weep.

"Pontmercy," said Marius, turning pale.

"Exactly, Pontmercy," says the priest. "Did you know him?"

"Monsieur," says Marius, "he was my father."

The priest lights up. "Well! Poor child, you can say you had a father who loved you dearly."[4]

Second, suddenly seeing his father in a whole new light, Marius investigates further. At a law library, he realizes what a war hero the man was and how his father's views of the world were so similar to his own. "Marius came to fully understand this rare, sublime, and gentle man, this lion-lamb who was his father," writes Hugo. "And how the two of them looked at the world almost as if one." To his grandfather's chagrin, Marius sheds his royalist political beliefs to align with his father's Napoleon tradition. "Napoleon became to him the people-man as Jesus is the God-man."[5] Later, he will join with the students hatching the antigovernment uprising of 1832.

If his father were still alive, Marius can imagine himself as a prodigal son. "If God in his mercy and goodness had allowed his father to be still alive, how he would have run, how he would have hurtled, how he would have cried out to his father, 'Father! I'm here! My beliefs are the same as yours! I am your son!'"[6]

It is the same way for the wanderers in the spiritual wilderness, the faith explorers, the God seekers. We show up at the door, feeling so out of place that we drop our hats to pretend we're remorseful. But hearing the story—the manger, the cross, the love—we realize for the first time: *this lion-lamb is my Father.* And when we investigate further, we see Him in a way we've never understood Him before. We thought He was distant, the celestial cop, the judge of wrath, only to find that He is grace personified and has loved us all the time. He kept His eyes on us even when we didn't know it. He wept because of the gulf between us.

And so we fall in love with Him for the first time. Understand Him for the first time. Feel the freedom for the first time.

Why? Because now we've heard the truth: some of it in stories told by others, some of it by daring to explore more deeply ourselves. "And the truth," says John 8:32, "will set you free."

POLITICAL OPINIONS
ARE UNWORTHY IDOLS

Certainly I approve of political opinions, but there
are people who do not know where to stop.[1]

—A PRIEST WHO BEFRIENDED GEORGES PONTMERCY

IT IS A BRIEF CONVERSATION BETWEEN MARIUS AND THE priest who had been so close to his father. It happens soon after Georges Pontmercy's death. It offers a subtle but increasingly important lesson to us: instead of resting in our faith in God, we can allow political persuasions to subtly rule our lives.

The priest, at this point, does not know the connection between Marius and the young man's "poor, brave father" he has come to know. "They were kept apart by political opinions," the priest tells Marius. "Certainly I approve of political opinions, but there are people who do not know where to stop. Just because a man was at Waterloo doesn't make him a monster; a father is not separated from his child for that."[2]

Sometimes politics becomes more important to us than the people on the other side of the political divide. We can so ardently define ourselves—and those around us—by political stances that we forget the deeper things beyond. Our unspoken mode of operation is not to get to know people different from us. Instead, it's to categorize them by their political persuasions—and label them as "good" or "bad" accordingly.

Isn't that what Gillenormand does with his son-in-law and his grandson? Isn't that the barrier that factures their relationships?

In some ways, we make politics an idol that deters, rather than enhances, our chance to be salt and light. Writes C. S. Lewis:

> A sick society must think about politics, as a sick man must think about his digestion: To ignore the subject may be fatal cowardice for the one as for the other. But if either comes to regard it as the natural food of the mind—if either forgets that we think of such things only in order to be able to think of something else—then what was undertaken for the sake of health has become itself a new and deadly disease.[3]

When we put too much weight on the political bridge, it's impossible to cross over and build relationships with those who see the world differently than we do. Why? Because we don't see others as individuals with strengths and weaknesses just like us; we see them instead as friends or foes, good guys or bad guys, right or wrong, based only on their political leanings.

We do the same with spiritual leanings. I already wrote about the student who pigeonholed me as bad news because I worked at a newspaper, her discernment based on the fact that, as she told me, "I'm a *Christian*." Conversely, I remember a supposedly open-minded editor who, prior to a meeting of other editors including me, read aloud a barbed letter written by a Christian about a political issue. The letter to the editor was undeniably etched with vindictiveness, not the kind of letter Jesus would write. I was, frankly, ashamed of what the man had said.

"Well," said the editor to half a dozen other editors in the room, "that's a *Christian* for you."

Really? She honestly believed that this man represented all Christians? The Christians I worked beside in Haiti, folks who'd paid two thousand dollars and flown to the poorest country in the Western Hemisphere so they could serve in a makeshift medical clinic from dawn to dusk, then perhaps awaken in the middle of the night to help a Haitian woman with an emergency C-section delivery? The guy I know who spends his days making and handing out sandwiches to the poor from the tailgate of his pickup truck? The twenty-six hundred volunteers who fanned out to forty schools in our community to do everything from pulling weeds to stripping and waxing floors because nobody else would step up to help our financially strapped schools? All these folks were just like the letter-writer?

I did not want to embarrass the editor in front of colleagues. So later I met with her. I asked her if she considered herself an environmentalist. She said she did.

"Oh," I said, "then you must go around spiking trees to discourage loggers from cutting them down," referring to ecoterrorists who don't mind risking a logger's life—the spikes can be deadly when struck by a chainsaw—to make a political point.

"Of course not," she said.

"But don't you see? That's the same logic you applied to that man's statement, which, by the way, I, too, found mean-spirited. You assumed that all Christians must be like him. But I need to tell you: he's not the one I try to model my life after, nor do I think he's the one most Christians I know would care to model their lives after."

Such narrow-mindedness works both ways: I've seen people who care about the earth quickly labeled as "environmentalists" and passed off as wackos. It's easier to label someone than to get to know someone. And it's tempting to be drawn into political frays that get in the way of deeper purposes.

For three decades in our community, people battled over a cross on a hill that many believed was a church-state violation, which the courts ultimately ruled was. Would Jesus, who didn't fight His own unjust death on a cross, have spent thirty years fighting for a concrete cross on a hill? I don't think so. He had bigger fish to fry: the lost, the blind, the poor, the people who didn't need some man-made symbol in their lives to compensate for a lack of genuine faith, but did need God-breathed grace. Not the outside stuff, the inside stuff. Not the dead stuff, the Living Water.

"What we seem to have lost is something as simple as respect—for each other, for the earth, and for the kind of values that could hold us together," writes Jim Wallis in *The Soul of Politics*.[4]

What turns Marius against a father he hardly knows is his grandfather's political pride that precludes the grandfather from seeing Pontmercy, his son-in-law, for the noble and gentle man he is.

What barricades does our own political pride erect? What enemies are we creating by seeing others not through God's "all fallen/all redeemable" perspective but through our more convenient political prisms? What bridges *aren't* we building to others because, when it comes to political opinions, as the priest says about Marius's father, we "do not know where to stop"?[5]

Lesson 36

JESUS' LIFE WAS
REVOLUTIONARY STUFF

If I die, let me die, let him live.[1]
—FROM JEAN VALJEAN'S SONG "BRING HIM HOME"

THE PHYSICAL CLIMAX TO *LES MISÉRABLES* IS STREET fighting based on an actual uprising that Hugo witnessed in June 1832. Some people believe the movie culminated in the French Revolution. No. That was a world-shaking revolution that took place from 1789 to 1794, complete with "Marie-Antoinette getting her head cut off; Madame Defarge knitting at the guillotine; and Napoléon somehow taking over at the end and cleaning up the mess," according to author and French Revolution expert Susanne Alleyn.[2]

"*Les Misérables*," she writes, "is, among many other things, about the *legacy* of the French Revolution. The uprising in the second half of *Les Miz* is no huge, nation-sized, world-shaking revolution like the 1789 biggie; it's a relatively small Parisian insurrection, a couple of days of street riots."[3]

The defiance against the royalist government was a reaction, writes Hugo, to "the three problems of the century—the degradation of man by the exploitation of his labor, the ruin of woman by starvation, and the atrophy of childhood by physical and spiritual night."[4] The violence was triggered by the death, from cholera, of a popular liberal politician and former Napoleonic general, Jean Maximilien Lamarque.

The uprising is a reminder of the passion that drives people to revolt. Among them: those who fought the Revolutionary War that led to the independence of the United States in 1776; those who seized power in the Russian Revolution in 1917 to establish the Soviet Union; and those who, during the 1950s and 1960s, joined what Martin Luther King Jr. called the "whirlwind of revolt" in the quest for equal rights for black Americans.[5]

Then, of course, there was Jesus, whom many today have relegated to a sort of "nice guy" and "cool teacher" status. Actually, He was far edgier than that. "Jesus was a total revolutionary," writes Dave Burchett in *When Bad Christians Happen to Good People*. "He granted status to women where none existed in the culture. His views were strange and upsetting to those in power . . . In that period of history, women were viewed as property. Divorce was a no-fault procedure for the husband only . . . And infanticide of baby girls was common in the Roman and pagan cultures."[6]

In addition, what made Jesus a revolutionary was His utter rejection of doing things the world's way with eye-for-an-eye justice, punish-thy-enemy focus. He rejected religiosity based on rules and championed, instead, the idea that everyone is redeemable. He didn't hang out in the royal palaces but with the riffraff, the ragamuffins, *les misérables*.

But what really made Jesus radical was the same thing that made the bishop of Digne radical. He was unlike others in His mercy and compassion. "Perhaps the most radical statement Jesus ever made is: 'Be compassionate as your Father is compassionate,'" writes Nouwen.[7]

You want radical? Jesus didn't only say love your neighbors, but love your enemies. "God calls His children to a countercultural lifestyle of forgiveness in a world that demands an eye for an eye—and worse," writes Brennan Manning.[8]

You want radical? Jesus said even looking at a woman lustfully is a form of adultery.

You want radical? Jesus asked the rich man to give it all up and come follow Him—just as Enjolras asks Marius to forget the trivialities of love and come join the revolution. "Citizen," Enjolras tells his friend after placing his hand on his shoulder, "my mother is the Republic."[9]

Jesus' Father is His Republic.

You want radical? Jesus, in Luke 9:48, says kings and generals and landowners with power and money and prestige aren't the greatest, but "he who is least among you all—he is the greatest." Today our world worships athletes, entertainers, and others whose pride in themselves oozes with every sound bite.

Consider Jesus saying, "Seek ye first the kingdom of God, and his righteousness, and all these things shall be added unto you" (Matt. 6:33 KJV). Jesus' words grind against the grain of popular thinking. "We find them the most revolutionary statement human ears ever listened to," writes Chambers. Why? Because they defy the status quo.

"But I *must* live, I *must* make so much money; I *must* be clothed; I *must* be fed," Chambers continues. "The greatest concern of our lives is not the kingdom of God, but how we are to fit ourselves to live. Jesus reverses the order: Get rightly related to

God first, maintain that as the great care of your life, and never put the concern of your care on other things."[10]

It means fighting against the mundanity of a material life. It means living not with follow-the-leader redundancy but with adventurous faith. It means eschewing a play-it-safe mentality for what Chambers calls "reckless joy,"[11] the idea of following our hearts to where God leads, despite the cadence of the culture around us.

In short, it means revolutionary living.

Lesson
37

THE TRUTH ISN'T
ALWAYS OBVIOUS

Marius almost reproached himself for his preoccupation
with his reveries and passion that until now had
kept him from noticing his neighbors.[1]

—*LES MISÉRABLES*

AFTER THE FALLING-OUT WITH HIS GRANDFATHER, THE once-well-to-do Marius finds himself on his own, living next to—quite literally—the riffraff of Paris in the Gorbeau House apartments. He gets to know a young woman from the family next door, Éponine. She and her family call themselves the "Jondrettes" as part of another identity-fraud scheme to bilk money from Valjean—not that Marius knew this.

"Every day at every moment, he heard them through the wall, walking back and forth, and yet he did not hear!" writes Hugo. "... He does not even listen, his thoughts are elsewhere on dreams, on impossible glimmerings, on loves in the sky, on infatuations; and all the while human beings, his brothers in Jesus Christ, his brothers to the people, were suffering agonies beside him."[2]

At this point in the story, discernment is not Marius's strength. Initially, Hugo writes, he is oblivious to his neighbors' poverty. Then he is slow to wake up to his neighbors' deceit. It is a lesson he learns—and I'm not endorsing his method—by peeping through a hole in the wall that separates his place from the "Jondrettes'."

When a "wealthy philanthropist" and his daughter—Valjean and Cosette—enter the room to offer help to this family desperately seeking it, Marius is too infatuated by the young woman's beauty to discern the deviously deeper meaning to all this.[3]

"Marius had not missed a thing in this whole scene, and yet he had actually seen nothing of it," writes Hugo. "His eyes had remained on the young girl, his heart had, so to speak, seized on her . . . Had the star Sirius entered the room he could not have been more dazzled."[4]

You get the idea. The peeping Marius is smitten, the brightness of this beautiful young woman blinding him to the insidious truth that is unfolding: the "Jondrettes" are actually the former innkeepers from Montfermeil, the Thénardiers, who have assumed new identities in Paris with evil intent; their latest ploy is this attempt to ambush Valjean and his daughter with the help of some local hoods. (After Thénardier reveals his identity, Valjean denies having ever met him.)

Though Marius has no such context, the scales finally fall off his eyes. After the man and young woman leave, he hears the family's mother and father plotting an ambush—with help from others—when the two return later that night. They plan to rob, perhaps even kill, the man. "Now," he realizes, "it was into a viper's hole he had just been looking; he had a nest of monsters before his eyes."[5]

Finally, Marius awakens to the truth, this manifestation of

Matthew 7:15: "Beware of false prophets, who come to you in sheep's clothing but inwardly are ravenous wolves" (esv).

Sometimes the world comes as a wolf in sheep's clothing, and though what's going on may be obvious to others, it's not to us. We either miss the disguise entirely or happily pretend not to notice. We need to be discerning. That doesn't mean being so obsessed with being exploited that we shy away from the slightest risk to help others. The good Samaritan didn't run a background check on the man who'd been beaten, robbed, and left for dead.

It does mean not being so distracted by the allure of one thing—in Marius's case, Cosette—that we miss the more sinister side of what really might be unfolding.

Perspective

CHANGES THINGS

There is one spectacle greater than the sea: That is the sky; there is one spectacle greater than the sky: that is the interior of the soul.[1]

—*LES MISÉRABLES*

CONSIDER, IF YOU WILL, HOW SIMILAR MR. AND MRS. Thénardier's circumstances are to their son Gavroche's. They are part of the same family. They live in Paris in the same time period. They are poor. And there is little about which to be hopeful, particularly for Gavroche. In 1830, the average life expectancy of a bourgeois child was eight years; of a worker's, two. Gavroche is a "barefoot urchin," writes Hugo.[2]

So why are the husband and wife mired in misery while Gavroche lives a relatively happy existence? Why do they exploit others while Gavroche, for the most part, encourages others? Why are the mother and father enslaved by their circumstances while Gavroche uses his to propel him into a sort of a free-wheeling existence that is underscored by care for others?

Perspective. Though their circumstances are similar, their ways of looking at the world are totally different. To wit, Gavroche

- looks at life as an adventure. Gavroche doesn't see a world of poverty. He sees a world of freedom and possibility. When two "interlopers" get into a fight, he observes with intrigue. "He was," writes Hugo, "having a marvelous time."[3]

- does not slip into self-pity. "In this absence of affection," writes Hugo, "the child lived like those pale plants that spring up in cellars. He felt no suffering from this mode of existence." And this despite Hugo's assertion that "his mother loved his sisters;" the inference, of course, is that she does *not* love him.[4]

- is not obsessed with the idea that he needs more, more, more to be happy. He already is, even if he lives inside a giant statue of an elephant. (In real life, shortly after the turn of the nineteenth century, Napoléon hatched plans to have the elephant built to honor himself, though only a plaster model was in place at the time he lost the Battle of Waterloo in 1815. Nevertheless, Hugo worked the elephant into his novel.)

- values people. Quite the opposite of his parents, he "bore no ill will to anybody," Hugo writes.[5] His parents are jealous of Jean Valjean and the wealth he's accumulated; never mind that he has obtained that wealth after overcoming a youth mired in poverty and a young adulthood stuck in prison. He has it, so they want it. Meanwhile, when Gavroche discovers two hungry, abandoned children, he gets them food, not even realizing they are his younger brothers. "If I had children," he says, "I would take better care of them than that."[6] Later, he gives some of his own clothes to help a homeless woman survive a night's bitter cold.

- laughs at life. When the sky opens up to rain, he says, "If this continues, I withdraw my subscription."[7]

- notices what is going on around him. It is Gavroche who, amid the street battle, realizes that Javert has sneaked through the lines in disguise to spy on the student revolutionaries. (And, sadly, it is Gavroche who, as with all the revolutionaries but Marius, dies in battle.)

- finds purpose. When he joins forces with the young revolutionaries, Gavroche sees himself as a smaller part of a greater good.

- is content with who he is and, thus, sees no need, unlike his parents, to deceive.

Why Gavroche and his parents are so different is open to debate. But their similar circumstances and different approaches to life remind us that how we respond to our obstacles may be more important than the obstacles themselves.

I once wrote about a young man who told me, "I don't have a single happy childhood memory." He was beaten by his mother's boyfriends. Thrown into a lake to learn to swim. Punched by one of those boyfriends when he caught the man cheating at Monopoly. And had his dog thrown against a wall. It did not help that he was discriminated against because of his ethnicity; his mother was white, his father African-American and Native-American.

And yet he grew up to be a first-rate father himself, a great husband, and, to me, a wonderful friend. Certainly, his faith had much to do with that. But I have seen plenty of people who claimed a faith in God yet who, even with happy childhoods, live mired in bitterness and regret.

He excelled for many of the reasons Gavroche excels: Because he is a survivor. Because he refuses to let his circumstances define who he is. And, finally, because he holds the perspective that it isn't about him.

LOVE MEANS LETTING GO

*Of all things God has created it is the human heart that
sheds the brightest light, and alas, the blackest despair.*

—VICTOR HUGO

MARIUS AND COSETTE HAVE EYES FOR EACH OTHER, IF ONLY
from a distance. But soon, even that is more than Jean Valjean
can handle. Remember, he and Cosette have lived a cloistered life
together since she was eight. She is now a teenager; nearly a decade
has passed since their days in the convent. Beyond Javert, until
now Valjean has had nothing threaten the bond between him and
the young woman who has given his life a deeper meaning; the
convent, in particular, kept her "safe" from threats of suitors. But
now they are living in Paris, having left the convent.

Valjean is now sixty and happy, content that he needs nothing
but the bishop's encouragement working through him, God above
him, and Cosette beside him. "Loved by Cosette, he felt healed,
refreshed, satisfied, rewarded, crowned," writes Hugo.[1]

Marius, obviously, is a threat to that contentment, even if
the young man and woman, at this point, have not even begun

speaking to each other; instead, they are falling in love from afar: "Like the stars in the sky separated by millions of miles, they lived by gazing at each other."[2]

Still, that is enough to raise the ire of a man who possesses Cosette as his and only his. And, it's worth noting, a man who has never been in love himself, which makes it all the more difficult for him to understand Cosette's yearning for Marius.

"Jean Valjean," writes Hugo, ". . . detested this young man."[3] (In the 1998 movie version, he actually slaps Cosette in his anti-Marius anger, though the gesture takes his anger well beyond Hugo's description of it.)

The possibility of losing Cosette brings out a selfish side to Valjean that we have not seen since a decade earlier when he steals the bishop's silver and, soon thereafter, a coin from the little boy, Petit Gervais. And his bitterness raises questions that we can relate to today: Are we loving those we love only because of what they can bring to us or what we can bring to them? Do we want them to be happy and fulfilled, period, or happy and fulfilled only because of us? In short, do we love them enough to lose them, if that's where their hearts must take them?

A more lighthearted, pop-culture version of Jean Valjean might be actor Steve Martin as George Banks in *Father of the Bride*. The issue wasn't so much *whom* his daughter was marrying; it was simply that she was marrying. Leaving. And rather than see this transition from her perspective, he initially saw it only from his own.

I remember similar feelings when the older of our two sons was heading off to college. I knew intellectually that this was the right thing to happen. It's what happened when I was my son's age.

Still, I can remember the last few months craving to spend time with him and feeling wounded because I wasn't able to. Letting go wasn't easy.

But isn't that what parenthood is all about, from the minute the umbilical cord is cut to separate mother from child? Letting go. We take our children to school. Watch them drive away in a summer-camp bus. Watch them—while biting our fingernails—take the keys to our cars and drive away. Leave for college. Get married.

Some see their children leave in more painful ways—as prodigals abandoning much of what their parents taught them to be true. Or as children who die young. Letting go comes in all sorts of shapes and forms, but it is as necessary to the parenting experience as it is painful.

"Love anything and your heart will certainly be wrung and possibly be broken," writes C. S. Lewis. "If you want to make sure of keeping it intact, you must give your heart to no one, not even to an animal."[4]

But Valjean has known pain like few others; two decades in prison can do that to a man. And he has known the contentment of having Cosette at his side. Thus, as the Cosette-Marius relationship transitions from faraway glances to "one kiss, and that was all,"[5] he decides there is only one way to keep his heart intact: Valjean and Cosette will move to England. (The musical suggests Valjean's motive is to distance himself from Javert.)

For all his bishop-like goodness, Valjean's Achilles' heel is a possessiveness of Cosette. It's understandable—she's become his life—but still selfish. Ultimately, he comes to his senses and makes the sacrifice of his life to secure Cosette's joy. In my son-leaving-for-college scene, I did nothing so noble, but gradually accepted that this is the way life must be, regardless of whether it causes pain for those of us who are waving good-bye.

I was inspired by a quote from Hodding Carter Jr., the Pulitzer Prize–winning Mississippi editor. "There are two lasting bequests we can give our children," he writes. "One is roots. The other is wings."

Lesson 40

SELF-PITY MORPHS INTO SELFISHNESS

These two beings, who had loved each other so exclusively . . . were now suffering beside one another and through one another; without speaking of it, without harsh feeling, and smiling all the while.[1]

—HUGO, ON VALJEAN AND COSETTE

JEAN VALJEAN SEES MARIUS NOT AS A MAN BUT AS A WOLF about to pounce on its prey—in this case, Cosette. "What had he come for?" writes Hugo. "He came to pry, to sniff, to examine, to test; he came to say, 'Now, why not?' He had come to prowl around his, Jean Valjean's, life! To prowl around his happiness, to grab it and carry it off."[2]

The once-noble Valjean quickly sinks into the quicksand of self-pity. "After first being the most miserable of men, I'll be the most unfortunate; I'll have spent sixty years of life on my knees; I'll have suffered all a man can suffer; I'll have grown old without having been young, have lived with no family, no relatives, no friends, no wife, no children!"[3]

He brings "woe is me" to a whole new level. This isn't just his adopted daughter growing up and getting married. This is game over. "I'll lose my life, my joy, my soul," he laments.[4]

You can understand why the man might fear such a change in his life. Cosette has *been* his life. But though Cosette is young, Valjean has to realize that ultimately he will need to let her go.

Or maybe not. For a man who otherwise leans toward the saintly side, news of the tryst with Marius sends him into a quiet rage. Such is the power of self-pity, whose effect isn't just that it stymies the one locked in it, but that it cuts our ties to those around us and the One above us.

"No sin is worse than the sin of self-pity," writes Chambers, "because it obliterates God and puts self-interest upon the throne."[5]

At first glance, it may seem like mere disappointment in something not going our way. *I try so hard, work so long, but nobody appreciates me . . . I don't get thanked or invited or honored . . . Others get credit that I deserve.* But ultimately, it becomes not about us lamenting a loss but about *us*, period. Us clinging to something so tightly that we refuse to let go; us putting ourselves above others; us consumed by *us*.

"When we begin to say 'Why has this happened to me?' 'Why does poverty begin to come to me?' 'Why should this difficulty come, this upset?' it means that we are more concerned about getting our own way than in esteeming the marvelous deliverance God has wrought," writes Chambers.[6]

Self-pity taints how we see ourselves (as victims), others (as oppressors of us), and God (if He even exists, as the ultimate oppressor of us). Consider these lines from Fantine's "I Dreamed a Dream": "I dreamed that love would never die / I dreamed that God would be forgiving."[7] God *is* forgiving, but in her pain-born self-pity—and you can certainly understand that pain—she cannot see such goodness.

I've seen it myself, in the mirror, when I've pined for a book to be successful, and it wasn't. I've seen it in churches when people wrap themselves so tightly around ministries that when they leave, they morph into bitterness that renders them ineffective in being a positive influence on others. And I've seen it in the world at large, notably in professional athletes who, replaced by someone else in a lineup, spiral into temper-tantrum babies, at times obliterating Gatorade coolers with bats in the process.

In such moments, the ugly truth is this: That man thinks more of himself than of his team. That woman thinks more of herself than of her church. That fellow thinks more of himself than of his God or family or friends. And, in the case of Jean Valjean, that man thinks more of himself than of his daughter.

The apostle Paul handles disappointment well. "I have learned to be content whatever the circumstances," he writes in Philippians 4. "I know what it is to be in need, and I know what it is to have plenty" (vv. 11–12).

"You will never awaken self-pity in the Apostle Paul," writes Chambers. "You might starve him or imprison him, but you could never knock out of him that uncrushable . . . certainty of God."[8]

His secret? Looking beyond self and circumstances, which prevents us from sinking in the quicksand of self-pity.

THE OLDER ARE NOT
NECESSARILY THE WISER

I have come to ask your permission to get married.[1]
—MARIUS, TO HIS GRANDFATHER

MARIUS, IN SOME WAYS, IS YOUNG AND FOOLISH, AS MANY OF us were at his age. (And some of us, in ways, still are!) But Hugo shows us his emerging quiet character—and his grandfather's self-centeredness—in an obscure scene that doesn't get much play beyond the book.

When Marius learns that Jean Valjean wants to take Cosette to England, he doesn't run off with her. He doesn't angrily confront Valjean. He doesn't wallow in self-pity, too self-absorbed to do anything at all. Instead, he goes to his grandfather—the man who bullied his way into Marius's life as a surrogate father—and pleads for the man's blessing to marry her.

For those who naturally assume the older you get the wiser you become, Gillenormand is "Exhibit A" of why that's not always true. Though, inside, he esteems his grandson-turned-son, though he longs to "have opened his arms,"[2] his selfish pride wins out.

He begins by making Marius feel guilty for having left four years before. ("Have you seen the errors of your ways?" he asks.[3]) When Marius begs for the man's pity, he uses it only as ammunition to fire another salvo of guilt-producing bullets. ("Pity on you, monsieur! The youth asks pity from the old man of ninety-two?"[4]) He scoffs when Marius asks permission to marry and berates a young woman about whom he knows nothing other than her name. ("Pttt!"[5]) Finally, he sends Marius away with reminders that his politics are poor. ("Never, monsieur! never!"[6])

By now, Marius is a puddle of pain.

"Father!"

"Never!"[7]

Just when you think Gillenormand can't stoop any lower, he does so by proposing an alternative to marriage. "Ninny!" he huffs. "Make her your mistress."[8]

It is the same callous, upper-class snobbery that Tholomyès exhibits when getting Fantine pregnant and then leaving her by way of a prank, the idea that the lower class—and Gillenormand clearly believes Cosette qualifies—can be used as a play toy and discarded.

And here is where Marius's honorable character rises to the surface. Writes Hugo, "That phrase 'make her your mistress' entered the heart of the chaste young man like a sword. He rose . . . and strode firmly toward the door. There he turned, bowed profoundly before his grandfather . . . and said, 'Five years ago you outraged my father; today you have outraged my wife [to be]. I ask nothing more of you, monsieur. Adieu.'"[9]

Gillenormand pleads for him to return, but it is too late.

How many parents today could have patched up a broken relationship with a child had they welcomed home a prodigal instead of lectured him or her? How many marriages could have been saved had a spouse swallowed his or her pride? How many friendships could have been reborn had an offended party offered forgiveness?

Young or not, Marius takes the high road, a decision that will prove fortuitous in the future. And a decision that reminds us that character isn't about age, but, wherever we are in our lives, about the courage to do the right thing.

Hiding feelings
hampers relationships

*To the old man it was an insupportable and irritating
anguish, to feel so tender and so tearful inside,
while he could only be outwardly harsh.*[1]

—Hugo, on Gillenormand

"Oh! what a tangled web we weave," writes Sir Walter
Scott, "when first we practice to deceive."[2]

Imagine what may have come of Gillenormand's relationship
with his grandson had he said what he really felt about the young
man. Goodness, he loves Marius something fierce. But does
Marius sense that love? No. Because Gillenormand is about control and pride and a flimsy form of honor, all of which he allows to
trump showing the young man he cares.

"To tell the truth," writes Hugo, "Marius was mistaken as to
his grandfather's heart . . . M. Gillenormand worshiped Marius."[3]

Their relationship fractures not because the grandson suddenly does an about-face and embraces his estranged father's

Napoleonic politics. Forget governments and countries; the deeper reason is the grandfather's unwillingness to affirm the young man. And so, with neither recognizing deeper ties, the political barrier appears insurmountable.

Too many relationships falter not because of differences people might have between each other, but because people don't counter those differences with affirmations. They don't express in words unconditional commitments. They don't say what needs to be said.

Someone once gave me advice as a youth baseball coach: "Encourage a kid whenever you get the chance. Because that kid may never get a single word of encouragement at home."

I've led men's retreats from Seattle to Tampa Bay and can tell you that one of the biggest weaknesses for guys is reminding their spouses how loved they are. On occasion, I've passed out pads of sticky notes to each one and challenged them to encourage their wives once a week. To tell their spouses how they feel. Inevitably, the push back I get is a good-natured, "But you're a writer. That's easy for you."

My response? "Your wife couldn't care less. She cares about whether you love her. These are sticky notes, not four-hundred-page journals. She won't care if you misspell something or put a comma in a wrong place. Instead, she'll be wowed that you took the time to say something nice about her." I know, I tell them, because the inside of one of our kitchen cupboards is still covered with such notes from me and my sons to my wife, more than twenty years after we wrote them.

Don't assume someone knows how you feel about him or her. Say what needs to be said—before it's too late.

Lesson 43

WE CAN BREAK THE
CHAINS FROM OUR PASTS

She looked straight into Marius's eyes
and said, "I have the address."[1]

—ÉPONINE, TO MARIUS, REGARDING WHERE COSETTE LIVED

BY NOW, JEAN VALJEAN'S WILLINGNESS TO CHANGE HIS WAYS has been well documented; a man who was once desperate for a morsel of food just to save himself ultimately saves at least nine people. But there's another character who breaks from her past to save someone and can easily be overlooked: Éponine. Near the end, she emerges as one of the story's most tragic and heroic figures.

Éponine is reared in the same parental squalor as her little brother, Gavroche, and her younger sister, Azelma. As the Thénardiers' eldest daughter, she is the same age as Cosette when Fantine's daughter comes to join the family. Éponine emerges as a younger version of her mean-spirited mother. "[Madame] Thénardier was unkind to Cosette, and Éponine and Azelma were unkind, too," writes Hugo. "Children at that age are simple copies of the mother; only the size is reduced."[2]

Cosette and the two sisters comprise a sort of *Cinderella* relationship, the newcomer "continually ill-treated, scolded, punished, beaten," but the two other girls living "in one halo of glory!"—at least in their mother's eyes.[3] In reality, Éponine helps a thief who is in cahoots with her parents in their underhanded ways. She is described by some literary analysts as a "wretched creature."[4] When Marius meets her, she is hardly the bourgeois-esque type of woman his grandfather would prefer he marry; instead, she is a waif who has served a short time in prison because of involvement with a scheme of her father's.

But years later, after falling in love with Marius, we see a different Éponine, if not Cosette-soft, then certainly less harsh; perhaps redeemed by her relationship with Marius, even if it is unrequited love.

Though reluctant, she agrees to be a messenger between Cosette and Marius, creating an ironic twist. When the girls are young, Cosette is the proverbial "odd girl out"; here Éponine plays that role, her willingness to help tinged with regret that such efforts are eclipsing whatever chance she has with Marius. "Thanks to you," sings Marius in the musical, "I am at one with the gods / And Heaven is near."[5]

Éponine's obvious mixed feelings underscore a nobility in her that would have seemed unthinkable in her young, spoiled childhood. In the musical, her song "On My Own" amplifies her angst of hope clashing with hopelessness. She longs for Marius but knows she can't have him.

Nevertheless, instead of letting pity have its way, she puts her life at risk by agreeing to be a messenger between Marius and Cosette. Her newfound nobility crescendoes in the barricade battle when she takes a musket bullet to save the life of Marius— and, while dying, gives him the letter from Cosette that will seal Cosette and Marius's relationship.

"Greater love has no one than this: to lay down one's life for one's friends," says John 15:13. And yet this sacrificial act in *Les Misérables* comes from the "wretched creature" who had scorned Cosette as a little girl. From someone whose earlier trajectory suggests she'd be more apt to kill Cosette so she could have Marius for herself. From someone who would seem to be the female epitome of Javert's pessimistic line from the musical: "Men like you can never change."[6]

But change is—or should be—the hallmark of lives rooted in faith. If not, why would God be necessary? If we're fine as is, why bow to a savior? Why attend this church, join that small group, read this book, invest in that relationship?

In a former church I attended, a leader's bullying tactics had grown old. He sloughed them off with a lighthearted, "That's just who I am." Perhaps so, but he was also someone who had failed to appreciate that the life of a follower of Jesus must constantly be about change, about becoming less like us and more like Him. As soon as we say, "That's just who I am," we might as well be Jean Valjean as a lifetime convict or Javert as an unyielding legalist. Might as well quit exploring life or reading Scripture or asking questions, the idea being that the concrete has already dried and, like it or not, we are who we are. Might as well say, *How can I get any better?*

The man was asked to step down from his leadership role. The good news: Unlike some, he didn't leave the church or turn bitter or mope. He faced himself. Mellowed. And found new ways to serve—with none of the bullying tactics he'd used before.

Like Éponine, proof that people can change.

Indeed, we *must* change.

Opportunities to help shouldn't be wasted

A [shot] had broken [Marius's] shoulder blade; he felt that
he was fainting . . . At that moment . . . he experienced
the shock of a vigorous hand seizing him . . .[1]
—Les Misérables

When Gavroche delivers a note to Jean Valjean from Marius, our protagonist utters "a hideous cry of inward joy."[2] Marius fully expects to die in battle, it says. It is a good-bye letter to Cosette. Valjean's worries are over. Cosette will not be leaving him after all. All Valjean has to do is keep the note in his pocket and Cosette will never know what has become of young Marius.

Valjean's conscience spoils the celebration. That conscience quietly pleads for him to reconsider. He calls for his doorkeeper. Loads his musket. And heads for the street battle where Marius's fate lies.

It is vintage Hugo that he doesn't give away Valjean's intent as he heads for the barricade. Is he going to save Marius or to confirm that Marius has died? When he arrives, Marius is alive, but Valjean later sees him get wounded. Then Valjean has one final chance to check his conscience at the revolutionary door. He can, of course, pretend he doesn't notice Marius and try to save himself. But, no, that "vigorous hand seizing" Marius is Jean Valjean's. He catches Marius as he falls and drags him away.

Circumstances haven't changed; that's not why Valjean suddenly decides to save the man who has come between him and the one thing he loves most in the world, Cosette. What has changed is Valjean's perspective. When the gunk of selfishness falls from his eyes, he sees a bigger picture. Suddenly, he sings in the musical's "Bring Him Home," "he's like the son I might have known / If God had granted me a son."[3] (A song, incidentally, whose lyrics took all night to write; lyricist Herbert Kretzmer was mired in writer's block until a colleague said, "Sounds like a prayer to me"—and Kretzmer wrote it as such.[4]) To save the young man, Valjean drags him into and through the Paris sewer system, a task only slightly less arduous than reading Hugo's nineteen-page meanderings about the history of the maze of tunnels.

All of which leads to this question: What do we do with opportunities to help others—even if pursuing them might cost us something?

Even though he's created a chasm between himself and Cosette with his off-to-England idea, Valjean has an opportunity to reverse his me-first thinking. If the easy, convenient, and selfish path is to let Marius die, he chooses the hard, inconvenient, unselfish path instead.

I once wrote about a man in our community who had, for five years, played the role of Jean Valjean on *Les Misérables'* national tour, including more than a year on Broadway. However, once finished, in the late 1990s, he could not bear to see a production of the musical. "I can't," said Kurk Davidson, forty-three at the time. "It's like having a dog you really love for a long time and then having to take him to the pound. You don't want to see him again."[5]

But in 2003, something drew him to a North Eugene High production of it. He spent five bucks on a play for which people on Broadway had once paid ninety dollars, in part to see him as the lead. He fidgeted in his seat. "It's like surgery," he said. "The wounds are too fresh."

When word leaked backstage that he was in the audience—a cast member's mother knew Davidson—the actors were incredulous. *Really? In our town? At our high school? A big-time Jean Valjean?* "I was freaked out," said Steve Fargher, who was playing that role.

The cast was as nervous as Davidson. But then something amazing happened. The play began, and the former actor was mesmerized at the first-rate job the cast and crew did. "These kids," he later said, "exceeded all my expectations."

After the play, when director Al Villanueva asked if Davidson would come backstage, he wound up staying for three hours. With Villanueva's blessing, he offered vocal tips and answered question after question until 1:00 a.m. "Like an onion, we tried to peel away the layers to see who these characters really were," he said.

"He'd ask you questions so you'd think more about your part," said Fargher. "He said, 'How do you think a father would act if he were saying goodbye to his child for the last time?'"

"You would take in every strand of her hair and the way it falls across her face," Davidson told him, "and how her fingers feel in your hand. Because that would be your snapshot for eternity."

(A perception spot-on with a line by Hugo, when Valjean was on his deathbed: "He began to gaze at [Cosette] as if he would take a look that should endure through eternity."[6])

By request, Davidson sang "God on High" to the cast and crew with stunning precision and passion. "He wasn't doing this for himself," said Chelsea Mortenson, who played Madame Thénardier. "He was doing it for us."[7]

Before the next weekend's show, Davidson had found a better dress for Fantine, coached actors, and helped with hair and makeup. "Kurk raised the level of the show," said Villanueva. "He's been an amazing gift to us."

Turns out he needed them as much as they needed him. "It's been a very healing experience for me," he said. "Cathartic. A sort of closure."

All because, like the character he played, he took advantage of an opportunity to go where he was needed.

Love has a gritty
side to it

*The darkness grew denser around Jean Valjean. He
nonetheless continued to advance, groping in the obscurity.*[1]

—Hugo, on Valjean carrying Marius through the sewer

To read Hugo's description of Jean Valjean carrying Marius through the Paris sewer system is to be reminded of love at its grittiest, grimiest, gut level. Can you think of anything more repulsive than carrying what amounts to a corpse through streams of human waste, sometimes up to your chin, while rats scamper about?

What could be worse? Perhaps encountering one of France's more despicable human beings, Thénardier, along the way, which Valjean does. And having him accuse you of murdering the man whose life you're struggling to save—this while reminding you, "Pugh! You don't smell very good."[2]

Hugo describes the muck in the sewer as human "manure." "Jean Valjean felt the pavement slipping away under him. He entered the slime. It was water on the surface, mire at the bottom . . . Now the mud came up to his knees . . . He sank in deeper and deeper . . . Now he had only his head out of the water, and his arms supporting Marius."[3]

Finally, consider that the man Valjean is trying to save is the very man who threatens all his happiness; Marius, in essence, is his cross to bear.

That said, the purest, deepest love is more the stuff of wading through the darkness of a sewer system beneath the burden of another than it is flowers and butterflies and knights on white horses and Chanel No. 5 and sunset smiles. The stuff that's not clean and trendy, but gnarled and challenging.

"All noble things," writes Oswald Chambers, "are difficult."[4]

Hugo himself proved that when he wrote *Les Misérables*. It took him twenty years in conception and execution, and when published in 1862, he was in exile from his beloved France because of his opposition to the royalist government. To add salt to Hugo's wounds, his critics chastised him for making money for dramatizing the misery of the poor.

More than a century later, Cameron Mackintosh (producer), Alain Boublil (French lyrics), and Claude-Michel Schönberg (music) found themselves teetering on failure with the early response to the musical version of *Les Misérables*. "We're doing a musical show . . . and it's got 'Miserables' in the title," writes Mackintosh. "It's got 29 onstage deaths . . . It's largely about French history . . . there are no dance routines, no tap shoes, no sequins, no fishnets, no staircase, no big stars, no cowboys, no chimney sweeps, no witches, no wizards. Moreover, there's virtually no advance at the box-office and it's received thumbs-down reviews. How can it possibly succeed?"[5]

Within weeks, usually staid British audiences were regularly offering standing ovations, many people with tearstained faces. It would become the most popular musical in history.

If noble things are difficult, love is even more so. Jason Reynolds, a twenty-three-year-old man, died in our community recently. For more than two decades, his family came together to love and care for him. He had been born with a muscle-eye-brain disease and had a 95 percent chance of dying by his second birthday.

"Where are you going to put him?" a friend asked them at the time, as in: what group home or care facility?

The family decided the living room would be a good spot. That way they could keep an eye on him, and he could keep an eye on them. He seldom left the house. Jason never went to a day of school. He never walked or talked. For twenty-three years, virtually all Jason Reynolds did was kiss the ones he loved and wink and remind them that in a world that celebrates "doing," "achieving," and "acquiring," it is sometimes enough to just *be*.

How else do you explain the eight card tables in the Reynoldses' living room, each spread with dozens of photos of him that his folks, Alan and Gail, were preparing for their son's memorial service?

You want love at its deepest? That is it. It's in taking care of a boy whom many would have discarded. You want love at its deepest? It's in more than 100 businesses and 250 individuals contributing to an "extreme home makeover" done for the family—basically, a $400,000-plus house—largely because of Jason's special needs. You want love at its deepest? It's in Jason's brother, Joel, a graduate student at Emory University in Atlanta, who claimed he is who he is because of the brother who never said a word to him.

You want love at its deepest? Look beneath the surface, into the sewers of sacrifice that some people willingly wade for others. Down there, in the darkness and obscurity, that's where you'll find the real thing.

We matter more
than we know

*The delight we inspire in others has this enchanting
peculiarity that, far from being diminished like every other
reflection, it returns to us more radiant than ever.[1]*

—*Les Misérables*

Until the book's end, Marius has no idea that Jean
Valjean saved his life, much less the hell the man went through to
do so; through no fault of his own, he is oblivious to the heroic
rescue. Conversely, we never see Valjean dwelling on the influence he has on others. To him, sacrificing for others is simply
the air he breathes. We never get the idea that he is particularly
aware of how much he matters to those around him, but it is
clearly true.

One of the more inspiring lessons of *Les Misérables* is that we
matter more than we know.

Sometimes we change someone's life; the bishop does that for
Valjean. Sometimes we save someone's life; Éponine does that for

Marius. Sometimes we give meaning to those around us; Cosette does that for Valjean.

At times, those we've helped realize how we've helped and show their appreciation; Valjean certainly never forgets what the bishop has done for him. But such acknowledgments are exceptions rather than rules. Still, if good deeds often go unnoticed, that doesn't mean the doers of them haven't made a difference.

My college years were the most depressing of my life. I was a new believer suddenly alone—or seemingly alone—in an environment not only opposed to that faith but in some cases hostile to it. I was separated from the young woman with whom I'd fallen in love just before heading off to college. I was questioning my future as a journalist, questioning the value of school as a means to some unknown end, questioning lots of things. All while living alone and, beyond that young woman, having no real go-to friend, meaning I had nobody else to share my burdens with. And—records will prove this—I was being rained upon with a consistency and volume unmatched in Oregon's already well-saturated climatological history.

But each morning as I'd leave for class, I would see the following verse scrawled in longhand on a piece of notebook paper and taped, from the inside, to some guy's rain-streaked dorm window for all to see:

And why do you worry about clothes? See how the flowers of the field grow. They do not labor or spin. Yet I tell you that not even Solomon in all his splendor was dressed like one of these. If that is how God clothes the grass of the field, which is here today and tomorrow is thrown into the fire, will he not much more clothe you—you of little faith? (Matt. 6:28–30)

For an entire school year, those words were a huge encouragement to me. First, for how they reminded me that I was of great worth to God, a fact easily forgotten amid my depression. Second, for how they reminded me I wasn't totally alone. God cared. And so, apparently, did the kid who posted the verse. I never knew who this young man was, but I always felt a bit more assured in my faith—and less alone in the rain—because he took the time to post those verses.

But unless he's reading this book—and if you are, thanks for the inspiration, from a kid in University of Oregon's Young-Earl Hall, 1973–74—he'll never know that. In fact, with rare exceptions, we'll never know how much we matter to others. Still, we make far more of a difference in the world than we'll ever know: schoolteachers who may only occasionally get a "thanks" from a parent; nurses who comfort a family that's here and gone; pastors who spread the seeds of God's Word and see only a little of what may grow.

"Who are the people who have influenced us most?" asks Oswald Chambers. "Not the ones who thought they did, but those who did not have even the slightest idea that they were influencing us."[2]

I once headed up a team of high school students who helped our newspaper put out a youth page each week. Among them was a young man who was brilliant but troubled, the kind of kid who was going to either win on *Who Wants to Be a Millionaire?* or festoon his biology teacher's house in toilet paper after getting what he thought was an unfair grade.

As a junior, he announced he was quitting school. I pleaded with him to finish, but he said he was tired of being "made to kneel" by teachers who treated him like a little puppy, giving him dog biscuits to reward him for correct answers.

"But quitting isn't the answer," I said.

"It is for me," he said.

I told him about a fifteen-year-old kid I'd written about years before who'd become a cocaine dealer, and how when I asked him where he'd be in five years, he told me—straight faced—that he would own his own island. Instead, he was in his fifth prison.

The disgruntled student quit anyway. I felt like a failure. How come I couldn't get through to this kid?

Over the years to come, I heard reports here and there that he hadn't landed softly. Within a few years, he was jobless, homeless, and suicidal. He had been evicted from his apartment. I would never see him again.

A decade after he quit school, I'd all but forgotten him. Then one day I got a letter in the mail with an Ohio postmark. I'd been invited to a dinner in honor of his graduation from college.

He'd gone to live with his grandmother and turned his life around. He'd fallen in love with theater after watching—I kid you not—*Les Misérables*. And now he hoped to be—this is delicious—a biology teacher.

Why had he invited me, all these years later?

Because, he told me, I'd never given up on him. And when everybody else had, knowing that somehow helped him not give up on himself.

We matter. To God. To others.

More than we'll ever know.

RELIGION ISN'T
THE ANSWER

He did not study God; he was dazzled by Him.[1]
—HUGO, ON VALJEAN

HUGO DESCRIBES JEAN VALJEAN IN MANY WAYS. "RELIGIOUS"
is not one of them. He is true to his word. He is honest. He brims
with integrity. He gives to others. But he isn't religious.

Likewise with the bishop, for whom the stereotype "religious"
might seem an obvious fit. He isn't empowered by some sort of
organized set of spiritual beliefs, but by the absolute passion to
mirror the grace of God to all he meets. That said, I don't think of
him as particularly "religious."

Neither was Jesus. People too often think of Jesus and think of
rules and regulations. Of right and wrong. No, these are the things
of Inspector Javert, the heartless things, the Pharisee-cherished,
nose-in-the-air, good-deeds stuff. Jesus was never about such
things. He was about heart change. About allowing the Holy Spirit
to work through us as yeast leavens bread, so every fiber in our

beings is about not pompously being religious, but about humbly serving others to bring glory to Him.

Not about rules, but about relationships. Not about self-righteousness, but about admission of our unworthiness. Not about team pride—"We've got Jesus, yes we do; we've got Jesus, how 'bout you?"—but about personal repentance. And isn't that what makes Jean Valjean the man he is? It isn't his things-I-avoid list or his politics or any smug bumper stickers he might have slapped on his carriage.

"Many a soul begins to come to God when he flings off being religious, because there is only one Master of the human heart, and that is not religion but Jesus Christ," writes Chambers.[2]

In Luke 18:10–14, Jesus tells the parable about the Pharisee and the tax collector. In the culture of the day, the Pharisee is religion personified, the tax collector quite the opposite.

> Two men went up to the temple to pray, one a Pharisee and the other a tax collector. The Pharisee stood by himself and prayed: "God, I thank you that I am not like other people— robbers, evildoers, adulterers—or even like this tax collector. I fast twice a week and give a tenth of all I get." But the tax collector stood at a distance. He would not even look up to heaven, but beat his breast and said, "God, have mercy on me, a sinner." I tell you that this man, rather than the other, went home justified before God. For all those who exalt themselves will be humbled, and those who humble themselves will be exalted.

Jesus never exalted the religious. He exalted the real. The repentant. Like Valjean, the ragamuffins who had hearts for heaven.

TRUE REVOLUTION STARTS AND ENDS IN OUR HEARTS

You are free.[1]

—JEAN VALJEAN, TO JAVERT AFTER HE CUT THE
ROPES ON THE INSPECTOR'S WRISTS AND FEET

EVEN THOUGH HUGO'S SYMPATHIES CLEARLY LIE WITH THE revolutionaries in the June 6, 1832, uprising, *Les Misérables* doesn't glorify war or sugarcoat it. As head of the revolutionary band of students, Enjolras's execution of one of his own men for killing a citizen coats eye-for-an-eye justice with a chilling veneer. And as the army approaches, he orders Javert's execution with an icy, "The last man to leave this room will blow out the spy's brains."[2]

Hugo suggests that true revolution must begin, and end, inside our hearts with forgiveness and not on the streets with fighting. "Hugo illustrates how the most profound revolution takes place in our individual consciences," says a Penguin.com overview of the book. "How every moment we are faced with decisions to do right or wrong, and how to make in our hearts pitched battles against our own worst impulses. *Les Misérables* incites us to make the best fight of our lives the fight to become authentically good people and gives us hope that our efforts will not be in vain."[3]

The bloodshed at the barricade does not change the world. True change instead must come from the changed hearts of individuals, the best *Les Misérables* example, of course, being Jean Valjean.

Nowhere does his compassion for others blossom more brilliantly than when, while the battle rages elsewhere, he is alone in the courtyard with Javert after promising Enjolras he will kill the spy. Instead, Valjean lets him go. Given ultimate power, a gun against a helpless victim, Valjean does not use it. Given justification—Enjolras has given him orders—he sets the inspector free. Given the chance for revenge against the man who'd tormented him much of his life, Valjean refuses to take it.

Since his candlestick conversion, Valjean has lived the words of Philippians 2:3–4: "Do nothing out of selfish ambition or vain conceit. Rather, in humility value others above yourselves, not looking to your own interests but each of you to the interests of the others."

Here, then, is the ultimate test for him to live out verses 5–7 in that swath of scripture: "In your relationships with one another, have the same mindset as Christ Jesus: who, being in very nature God, did not consider equality with God something to be used to his own advantage; rather, he made himself nothing by taking the very nature of a servant."

In other words, given the power, do we use it to exploit, or do we use it to protect? Do we become tyrant or servant? Do we raise ourselves up in glorious triumph, or do we bow down to a higher calling?

Valjean bows. He cuts the rope to set Javert free, ignores Javert's plea to kill him—it would have ended the shame the inspector feels for having failed on his mission—and fires the gun into the sky to signify the execution has been carried out. By faking the execution of Javert, Valjean ensures that nobody else will kill the inspector. He saves the life of the man he fears most in the world.

This is a key moment in *Les Misérables,* the moment when Jean Valjean, in essence, becomes the bishop. It is as if his faith has ripened to its ultimate fruition.

Think about it: Isn't Valjean's cutting of those ropes the equivalent of the bishop freeing the former convict to start anew? ("I have bought your soul for God," read the lyrics from "The Bishop," a song from the musical.[4]) Isn't his gunshot "lie" the equivalent of the bishop lying to the police that he'd given the silverware to Valjean? And, finally, isn't Valjean's willingness to grant mercy to Javert the equivalent of the bishop saying, "Take the candlesticks too"? After all, in setting the inspector free, Valjean is risking that the man might turn on him, which is what subsequently happens.

Says Jesus, "Love your enemies, do good to those who hate you, bless those who curse, pray for those who mistreat you" (Luke 6:27–28).

In the twenty-first-century United States, our wars don't often spill into the streets. They're cultural wars, political wars, fought in Senate chambers, city council meetings, and in the minds of millions of people. And the good guy–bad guy divide on either side of the barricade sometimes comes down to Christians and non-Christians.

The only thing we seem to agree on is that America is not working. Drugs. Dysfunctional families. School violence. More people in prison than ever before. Both "sides" clamor for change. But if we, as believers, think we're going to "fix" this country from the top down, we're ignoring thousands of years of human history and Scripture. Real change must start from the bottom up, one changed heart at a time; people making decisions not to benefit self but others. "For not with swords' loud clashing, or roll of stirring drum; with deeds of love and mercy the heavenly kingdom comes," says the old hymn "Lead on, O King Eternal."[5]

Shouldn't we be more revolutionary, not in our politics, but in our daily lives? Our choices? Our time? Our love? Shouldn't we want to erect barricades to block us not from people who don't believe as we do, but from the trivial distractions that suck the God-life right out of us? And shouldn't we be filling it with the fruits of the Spirit as listed in Galatians 5:22–23: "love, joy, peace, forbearance, kindness, goodness, faithfulness, gentleness and self-control"?

Alas, with those who don't share our faith, we'd rather set up a barricade and go to war than magnify God's love through Valjean-esque action. "What makes the temptation of power so seemingly irresistible?" asks Nouwen. "Maybe it is that power offers an easy substitute for the hard task of love. It seems easier to be God than to love God, easier to control people than to love people, easier to own life than to love life."[6]

Jean Valjean is Hugo's "Jesus-man." And what does he do with his power? "Jesus emptied himself of power that was rightfully his," writes Cal Thomas and Ed Dobson in *Blinded by Might*. "We try to fill ourselves with power that belongs to the world and seek to usher in a kingdom not of this world by using tools that are of this world."[7]

The right man for president. Numerical advantages in the

House and Senate. A Supreme Court ruling. These are the things we think will tip the scales in our favor. But what will really impact the world for God's glory will be living with the selflessness of a Jean Valjean, who given a chance for power, instead "made himself nothing by taking the very nature of a servant."

THE LAW IS NOT ENOUGH

*The supreme happiness of life is the
conviction that we are loved.*[1]
—LES MISÉRABLES

JAVERT RELUCTANTLY ACCEPTS HIS FREEDOM, BUT RATHER than allow it to be a catalyst for personal change, quickly returns to the ruts of legalism. If only he brings Jean Valjean to the courts, the law will prevail. Justice will prevail. He will prevail. Alas, even after apprehending Valjean at a sewer exit and allowing him to take Marius home to his grandfather and to see Cosette one final time—even though he knows the spider has finally caught the fly, he anguishes in indecision.

Why? Because his entire life has been steeled in the Pharisee-like obsession to follow the law, and for the first time it appears the law is not enough. He realizes—oddly, with shame—that he, too, has a heart. Why else would he have allowed Marius to be taken to his grandfather?

But rather than see his softening as a strength, he sees it as the ultimate weakness. He is consumed by a sense of failure, confused by Valjean's compassion, and confounded by his own lack thereof. He knows Valjean is not innocent, but he is *good*, and for the first time Javert seems to recognize that. He cannot arrest the man, but neither can he live with himself for not doing so. Years before, when he thought he'd wrongly accused Madeleine of being Jean Valjean—when he'd failed—he immediately offered his resignation. Now, for what he sees as another failure, the only resignation he thinks he can offer is his life. He throws himself into the raging Seine River.

Valjean and Javert are similar men, both raised in poverty, both loners, both clinging to unshakable ideals, both driven to making a difference in the best ways they know how. What separates them is this: When shown grace by the bishop, Valjean allows that undeserved favor to transform himself into a new man. He embraces it. And when shown grace by Valjean, Javert rejects that favor. He flees from it.

Valjean is about change; Javert about refusing to change. Valjean is about going from a slave to a free man; Javert about staying a slave to self. Valjean is about compassion; Javert about creeds, even if he ascribes a certain religiosity to his creed. ("Mine is the way of the Lord," he gallantly sings in the musical's "Suddenly."[2]) Valjean sees his soul's inner sickness and allows himself to get well; Javert senses that sickness and dares not treat it. Valjean is about resurrection, Javert about rebellion.

For one man, mercy leads to life. For another, mercy leads to death. Each makes his choice. Valjean not only considers the question raised in the song "Valjean's Soliloquy" from the musical, "Is there another way to go?" He acts on it: "Another story must begin!"[3] Javert doesn't dare consider that there might be another way to go; his song "Javert's Suicide" mirrors the music of Valjean's

"Soliloquy" but the lyrics speak of hopelessness: "There is nowhere I can turn / There is no way to go on!"[4]

What kills Javert in the end is pride: his absolute belief that his way—the law—is the answer. When he realizes that which he's trusted has failed him, he has only two choices: swallow that pride and allow grace to reshape him, or wrap himself in that pride as a death robe and take it to his watery grave.

You live by the law, you die by the law. Solzhenitsyn, the Russian writer and dissident who was imprisoned for eleven years, says, "A society which is based on the letter of the law and never reaches any higher is taking very scarce advantage of the high level of human possibilities."[5]

He isn't saying to do away with the law. He is saying that there's something more. When we believe otherwise—when we put an entire society's weight or even our individual weight on the law and only the law, it is not strong enough to hold us. And we, too, plummet into our personal Seines, be they addictions, obsessions, or other escapes where, as the song from the musical says, "the stars are black and cold."[6]

"When only the law and politics arbitrate human affairs, everything becomes political—even the most basic human relations," writes Don Eberly in *Restoring the Good Society*. "The law begins to resemble a harried referee who has the impossible task of policing a sport that is both choked by rules and overwhelmed by infractions. The pursuit of a just society is reduced to fighting over the rules."[7]

Why? Because people don't see the bigger picture that, consciously or subconsciously, we crave. That's why Jesus rebuked the letter-of-the-law Pharisees. Like Javert, their passion for dotting the *i*'s and crossing the *t*'s became more important than the substance of whatever story they were writing. They would respect the Do Not Swim sign more than the drowning child they refused to save.

"Their zealotry obscured the way of God," writes Thomas and Dodson in *Blinded by Might*. "They had focused so much on God's law that they completely missed the ultimate objective—which was not a legalism no person could live up to, but a redemption that God had stooped down to accomplish."[8]

We can cling to legalism, yes. But just as it betrays Javert, it will not hesitate to betray us.

LOVE PERSEVERES

*The spirit does not give way to despair until it has
exhausted every possibility of self-deception.*[1]

—*LES MISÉRABLES*

IT IS 1833, EIGHTEEN YEARS SINCE JEAN VALJEAN HAS BEEN
released from prison. He is sixty-four, even if the 2012 movie
version makes him look even older. Marius and Cosette marry.
But Valjean—and the musical doesn't go here—senses he can
no longer keep his past a secret. In the novel, before the wedding,
Valjean—ever the stickler for doing right—fakes an accident with
his writing hand to avoid having to forge a false name on the marriage certificate, then goes to Marius to confess his criminal past.

Initially, Marius doesn't believe Valjean. When Marius finally
accepts the truth of Valjean's statement, the young man offers to
arrange for a pardon, but Valjean refuses. They agree that Valjean
will see Cosette only in the evenings. Marius later begins questioning Valjean's honesty because he believes he executed Javert on the
barricade and doubts Cosette's dowry was amassed legitimately.

Gradually, Marius pushes Valjean out of Cosette's life. Valjean grows ill and begins facing his impending death.

You could argue that this wouldn't have become so messy had Valjean simply told the rest of the story, that it was he who dragged Marius's nearly dead body through the sewer and saved his life. And that although Marius believes Valjean killed an innocent man—Javert—in cold blood during the revolution, it is Valjean who actually gives the police inspector his freedom before the man kills himself.

But Valjean has never lost the unworthiness branded into him as a convict. He has always been far better at standing up for others than at standing up for himself. Since his encounter with the bishop, he has tried to simply do the right thing—and let the chips fall where they may. Though his will to live wanes, his love for Cosette persists. Though so heartsick at this new divide that he gives up on life, he does nothing to come between Cosette and Marius for his own benefit as, say, Gillenormand, has done by driving a wedge between the boy and his father.

"Love does not delight in evil but rejoices with the truth," says 1 Corinthians 13. "It always protects, always trusts, always hopes, always perseveres" (vv. 6–7).

In an ironic twist, Hugo brings in none other than Thénardier to make things right. Disguised as a statesman with important information that he is willing to—why, of course!—*sell* to Marius, he tells all: About Valjean having been "Mayor Madeleine" and having made considerable money at the factory in Montreuil-sur-Mer, meaning Cosette's dowry is indeed legitimate. About Javert not being murdered by Valjean but killing himself. And most important—ironically, to convince Marius that Valjean was carrying a man he murdered through the sewer—about a fragment of fabric

Thénardier had taken from the dead man's coat to prove it. (In the musical it is a ring.) But when Marius recognizes the fabric as taken from his own coat, the real truth is unveiled: the man Valjean was carrying through the sewer was him. It was Valjean who had saved Marius that night.

Though Cosette has never doubted Valjean's goodness, the revelation seals Jean Valjean with nobility in the eyes of Marius—in his eyes, writes Hugo, "the convict was transfigured into Christ."[2]

Love perseveres.

I picture a living room full of people I recently sat among for a story about a support group for families with relatives in prison. They were a cross-section of our community: A banker. A Realtor. A retired schoolteacher. Protestants. Catholics. Unitarians. People wearing Birkenstocks. A woman who drove a Lexus. A college student. All bound by something that, if they were not ashamed of, they didn't particularly want others outside the room to know: each of them had a loved one in prison: a son, a daughter, a grandson, a husband, a father. And their love for that person persevered despite the darkness of the situation. Despite the complexities. Despite the muck of the sewers.

I picture one of those people in particular, a friend of mine whose son made some poor choices when he was young. He was sent to prison. I picture my friend across the table from me at numerous lunches we had together over the years, talking enthusiastically about his son's progress. Sorry about his son's mistake but steadfast in his unconditional love for him.

Finally, I picture the recent summer day we sat outside for lunch and our waiter, a handsome, good-natured young man, came to our table. It was his son. He had been released from prison.

Despite the cold shoulder of a society that's not quick to forgive, he was building a new life, partly on the strength of a father who wouldn't give up on him.

Love always trusts, always hopes, always perseveres.

We are *les misérables*

When philosophy fathoms the facts to which they correspond,
it often finds in them many grandeurs among the miseries . . .
the impoverished made Holland; the populace more than
once saved Rome; and the rabble followed Jesus Christ.[1]
—*Les Misérables*

The end of the 2012 movie version of *Les Misérables* is the most emotional cinematic experience I've had; it's the first time I've been in a post-film restroom with guys whose common experience wasn't just relieving their bladders but blinking back tears while trying to still act semi-macho.

You have Jean Valjean's swan song ("God on high, . . . bring me home . . ."). You have Marius and Cosette, she learning from her new husband that her father saved his life. You have, of course, a special guest appearance by Fantine (". . . chains will never bind you"). You have Valjean's symbolic death and reach for heaven, walking through the candle-imbued church to the bishop, Myriel's hand outstretched in welcome ("To love another person is to see the face of God"),[2] all of which segues into an aerial shot of Éponine and Gavroche and Enjolras and the other revolution-aries who died in their pursuits of freedom, singing from atop the barricade ("For the wretched of the earth / There is a flame that never dies . . .").[3]

As you look back at the grandeur of Hugo's story, you realize the glory of *Les Misérables* is its universal theme. Go anywhere and you will find the same tragedy, the same injustice, the same poverty. Go anywhere and you will find a search for redemption, for reconciliation, for love. Go anywhere and you will find the downtrodden.

"So long as ignorance and misery remains on earth," writes Hugo, "books like this cannot be useless."[4]

In our subconscious life-dramas, we may fancy playing the part of the Paris bourgeois, but we're better fits for the streets-of-Digne Jean Valjean or the desperate Fantine or the letter-of-the-law Javert, who is contentedly attired in his moral straitjacket. We're all *les misérables* trying to find ourselves. As Enjolras sings in "ABC Café/Red and Black": "It is time for us all / To decide who we are."[5]

Or, at life's barricade, time to decide with whom we will link arms. "At issue," writes Nouwen, "is the question: 'To whom do I belong? To God or to the world?' Many of my daily preoccu-pations suggest that I belong more to the world than to God. A little criticism makes me angry, and a little rejection makes me depressed. A little praise raises my spirits, and a little success excites me. It takes very little to raise me up or thrust me down. Often I am like a small boat on the ocean, completely at the mercy of the waves."[6]

"Who am I?" The question Valjean struggles with on the night before the trial for Fauchelevent is the very question with which we, too, wrestle. Ultimately, he decides, "I am God's." But that is easier said than done in a world that tells us we are what we wear, where we live, how much we make.

It's deliciously ironic that Susan Boyle—a middle-aged, frumpy-looking Scottish woman who hadn't sung much beyond karaoke pubs and her Catholic church before appearing on *Britain's Got Talent* in 2009—made it big by singing "I Dreamed a Dream" from *Les Misérables.* Her subsequent album became the United Kingdom's bestselling debut album of all time. Her life literally changed overnight. It's almost as if she became the living embodiment of hope for the hopeless. And when she was asked to perform at Windsor Castle, the invitation echoed of Fantine's daughter and her "Castle in the Sky" dream. The cynics may see only Boyle's fame and fortune as her rewards, but her autobiography suggested that far more meaningful to the singer was this: affirmation in a world that had given her little, in fact had bullied her. *You're deserving . . . You're worthy . . . you're honorable . . .*

Aren't such words the longing of every street urchin, every ragamuffin, every never-good-enough misfit as so defined by a culture that can be so caustic? The kind of people Jesus embraced without restraint, like the thief hanging on the cross next to him to whom He says, "Truly I tell you, today you will be with me in paradise" (Luke 23:43)?

Jesus chose an unlikely group to spread His all-important message to the world: Shepherds. A few fishermen. A tax collector. And ultimately, *us.*

In the same vein, at the end of *Les Misérables,* who winds up with the handsome prince and his family's "castle in the sky"? Cosette, of course, who, in the eyes of many in nineteenth-century France, is nothing but—let's use the word as it was originally intended—a bastard. A waif. A child slave.

Challenged by an agnostic to tell the Christian message in ten words, Will Campbell, a Yale Divinity School graduate and former director of religious life at the University of Mississippi, said it like this: "We are all bastards but God loves us anyway."[7]

Yes, we—*les misérables.*

Lesson 52

To love another person is to see the face of God

It is nothing to die; it is horrible not to live.[1]
—Jean Valjean, to Cosette and Marius on his deathbed

Hugo offers hints but ultimately leaves it up to the reader to decide why, at sixty-four, Jean Valjean dies. He writes that Valjean is like "a pendulum that has not been wound up, and whose oscillations are growing shorter before they stop . . . Youth goes where joy is . . . Old age goes to its end."[2] The suggestion? That Valjean is dying of old age. Meanwhile, though, he hints that Valjean's refusal to eat might be related to life without Cosette. "His countenance expressed this single idea: What is the use?"[3] The suggestion? That he might be dying of a broken heart.

"What is the matter with him?" his concierge asks the doctor.

"Everything and nothing," he says. "He is a man who, to all appearances, has lost some dear friend. People die of that."[4]

Less important than how Jean Valjean dies is how he lived—and how the life he lived reconciles him to his death. "I am," he tells Cosette and Marius, "dying happy."[5]

Certainly he is racked with bitterness without Cosette. But when she and Marius embrace him in the end, he delights in his realization that they've forgiven him his criminal past.

That said, why shouldn't he die happy? He's overcome myriad obstacles to live an honorable life. He's gone from convict to triumphant hero. He's made good on the bishop's encouragement "to become an honest man." He's completed the promise he made to Fantine to take care of Cosette. He's eluded Javert. And after Marius and Cosette find out the whole truth, he has been affirmed by both. "Oh!" he says. "It is good to die like this!"[6]

Death is always sad. But Valjean's passing bears little of the hopelessness of the "empty chairs at empty tables" lines after the barricade battle. Despite sinking into despair when separated from Cosette, Valjean dies bathed in the warmth of her love, having long ago come to grips with her need to strike out on her own with Marius. Why else would he have gone to the lengths he did to save the young man who becomes her husband? For *her*. For what he realizes would be her inevitable "leaving and cleaving" with someone new, even if it is painful for him to let go in the process.

Long ago, I saw a television program in which a group of one-hundred-year-old people were asked how, if given the chance, they would live their lives differently. They said three things:

First, they would take more risks. Valjean's entire life is a risk, beginning with his daring to knock on the door of the bishop's house. For decades, he continually risks his life, his reputation, and his comfort—and, admirably, not for himself but for the benefit of others.

Second, they would enjoy the journey more while they were on it. Certainly, Valjean's life is a tapestry of tragedy and triumph, but once he has his encounter with the bishop he understands—and appreciates—grace for the first time. And once Cosette enters his life he understands—and appreciates—love for the first time. "His whole heart melted in gratitude," Hugo writes, "and he loved more and more."[7] That sounds like someone enjoying the journey.

Finally, the centenarians would invest more deeply in that which would outlast them. In other words, they'd concern themselves more with their legacies. Valjean writes a letter—"my last confession," he sings in the musical—to Cosette. He bequeaths her the candlesticks, the symbol of commitment to a new life lived in honor of the bishop who saved his life. He even leaves a tidy financial legacy.

But, more important, he leaves a *model* for her and Marius of how to live life at its deepest: Rescuing her from the Thénardiers. Rescuing Marius from almost certain death. And yet doing so with unmistakable humility. "I do not know whether he who gave [the candlesticks] to me is satisfied with me in heaven," he says. "I have done what I could."[8]

Not only done what he could, but left an honorable legacy made all the richer because of the convict's life he overcame to reach such honor. That's the hopefulness of *Les Misérables* some cynics have ignored, the idea that the individual can rise above the cultural darkness and make a difference. Group violence at the barricade does not change the world; Valjean, through individual integrity invested in the people around him, does.

In the end, he reconciles with the one life that matters to him more than the others: Cosette's. He reminds her of their first meeting in the dark of the woods that night, of the doll he gave her. He talks of God. ("He knows what He does in the midst of His great stars."⁹) He even encourages Cosette and Marius with the biblical command to forgive their enemies, specifically the Thénardiers.

His final remembrances, it's worth noting, are not about positions he's held or things he's accomplished or honor he's been given—all of which he is worthy. Instead, his final remembrances are about relationships, which is appropriate given the life he's led.

Think about it. What turns Jean Valjean's life around isn't some secret code to fulfillment that the bishop had given him. It isn't—á la Javert—a set of rules. It isn't religion. What turns his life around is this: a relationship.

Ironically, it is a Pharisee—a biblical Javert, "an expert in the law" (Matt 22:35)—who asks Jesus the key question along such lines: "Teacher, which is the greatest commandment in the Law?" (v. 36). Translated: *What's the meaning of our lives? What's it all about? What really matters?*

"Love the Lord your God with all your heart and with all your soul and with all your mind," Jesus says. And "love your neighbor as yourself" (vv. 37, 39).

God. People. Relationships.

This is why He came. This is why we exist. This is the stuff Valjean has in mind when he says on his deathbed, "It is nothing to die; it is horrible not to live."¹⁰ Horrible, he suggests, to not have invested in others. To not have made connections with people a priority. To not have "left it all on the field," as Valjean has clearly done.

In Matthew 25, Jesus tells the story of a king who says, "For I was hungry and you gave me something to eat, I was thirsty and you gave me something to drink, I was a stranger and you invited me in, I needed clothes and you clothed me, I was sick and you looked after me, I was in prison and you came to visit me" (vv. 35–38).

In other words, "I was among *les misérables*—and you were there for me."

The people don't get it. They don't recall ever having provided such comfort to Him. But He replies, "Truly I tell you, whatever you did for one of the least of these brothers and sisters of mine, you did for me" (v. 40).

The musical translates it beautifully, this idea that life lived to its fullest is manifested in reaching out to those around us, which in turn is a reaching up to God: "To love another person is to see the face of God."[11]

As we wander our personal streets of Digne, isn't that what we long for to fill our hunger for meaning? The nourishment of the stuff that lasts? The sustenance of the significant? The goodness of grace?

"Madame Magloire," I can almost hear the bishop saying, "another place please."[12]

BOOK CLUB QUESTIONS

1. If you could choose one of the fifty-two lessons that hit home with you, which would it be, and why?

2. Have you ever had a stranger metaphorically "knock on your door" as the bishop did with Jean Valjean? How did you react and why? Would you do the same if the opportunity presented itself again?

3. Of the characters in Victor Hugo's novel, whom do you relate to most, and why?

4. How were Jean Valjean and Javert similar? How were they different?

5. Hugo wrote about how people "confuse heaven's radiant stars with a duck's footprint left in the mud."[1] In what ways do we do that?

6. Welch asserts that "crisis reveals character." Why and how?

7. Who emerged as your personal hero in *Les Misérables*? Who did you despise?

8. In what ways do you believe nineteenth-century France and twenty-first-century America are culturally similar? How are they different? What can we learn from the historical past?

9. If you could immerse yourself in only one version of *Les Misérables*, which would it be: the book, the musical, or one of the many movies? Why?

10. Choose someone in your life who resembles one of the characters from *Les Misérables*. What have you learned from this person?

11. In what ways does the church today promote values that are aligned with Jean Valjean's? That are aligned with Javert's?

12. What similarities do the rich and poor share?

13. Jean Valjean agonized over letting go of Cosette. Whom or what was difficult for you to let go of? What did you learn from the experience?

14. Name one of the author's lessons of which you're skeptical. Why? What would be a better variation of that lesson?

15. What's your favorite moment in *Les Misérables*, and why?

Acknowledgments

THANKS TO SALLY JEAN WELCH, WHO "DREAMED THE DREAM" for this book—and who encouraged me on the journey. To Mollie Petersen (that French-reading niece) and Ann Petersen, who kept my feet to the accuracy fires. (Though I take responsibility for any mistakes that remain.) To Al Villanueva, Judy Wenger, Deena Welch, Sally Jean Welch, Dean Rea, and Lou Rea, for other expert editing. To Kristen Parrish of Thomas Nelson, who guided the project so proficiently. To all the actors and actresses who so vividly brought Hugo's story to life for me. And, finally, to my neighbor across the street, who, as I was writing each morning, revved up his pickup precisely at 6:00 a.m. to give me that extra jolt I needed to carry on for *one day more*.

ABOUT THE AUTHOR

BOB WELCH IS THE AUTHOR OF SEVENTEEN BOOKS, AN AWARD-winning columnist, a speaker, and an adjunct professor of journalism at the University of Oregon in Eugene.

He has won dozens of journalism honors, including the *Seattle Times* C. B. Blethen Award for Distinguished Feature Writing, and is a multiple winner of the National Society of Newspaper Columnist's best-writing award.

His articles have been published in inspirational books, including the popular *Chicken Soup for the Soul* series and magazines such as *Reader's Digest*, *Sports Illustrated*, *Runner's World*, and *Focus on the Family*.

Welch speaks nationwide and is the founder and director of the Beachside Writers Workshop in Yachats, Oregon.

He and his wife, Sally, have two grown sons and five grandchildren.

Notes

Author's Note

1. Graham Robb, *Victor Hugo: A Biography* (New York: W. W. Norton, 1999), 379.

2. Victor Hugo, *Les Misérables*, trans. Frederick Charles Lascelles Wraxall, vol. 3 (London: Hurst & Blackett, 1862), 219.

3. Edward Behr, *The Complete Book of Les Misérables* (n.p.: Arcade, 1993), 39–42.

4. Victor Hugo, *Les Misérables: A New Unabridged Translation*, Signet Classics reissue, trans. Lee Fahnestock, Norman MacAfee, and Charles Edwin Wilbour (New York: Penguin, 1987), 518. (Hereinafter Hugo, *Les Misérables: A New Unabridged Translation*.)

5. Benedict Nightingale and Martyn Palmer, *Les Misérables: From Stage to Screen* (Milwaukee: Applause Theatre & Cinema Books, 2013), 37.

6. Ibid.

7. Edwin Percy Whipple, "*Fantine*, by Victor Hugo: A Review by Edwin Percy Whipple," *Atlantic Monthly*, July 1862, available at http://www.theatlantic.com/past/docs/unbound/classrev/lesmisfa .htm.

Notes

Lesson 1

1. Hugo, *Les Misérables: A New Unabridged Translation*, 15–16.
2. Ibid., 106.

Lesson 2

1. Hugo, *Les Misérables: A New Unabridged Translation*, 57.
2. Ibid., 1, 53.
3. Ibid., 1.
4. Ibid., 52, 53.
5. Ibid., 10, 13–14.
6. Ibid., 15.
7. Ibid., 50–51.

Lesson 3

1. Hugo, *Les Misérables: A New Unabridged Translation*, 69.
2. Ibid.
3. Henri J. M. Nouwen, *The Return of the Prodigal Son: A Story of Homecoming*, reissue ed. (New York: Image Books/Doubleday, 1994), 42–43.

Lesson 4

1. Hugo, *Les Misérables: A New Unabridged Translation*, 26.
2. Ibid., 85.
3. Ibid., 74.
4. Ibid.
5. Ibid., 76.
6. Ibid., 71.
7. Ibid., 76, 77.

Lesson 5

1. Hugo, *Les Misérables: A New Unabridged Translation*, 110.
2. Ibid., 106.
3. Ibid.
4. Ibid., 110.
5. "The Confrontation," *Les Misérables Live! Dream the Dream* (2010

Cast Album, New 25th Anniversary Production), compact disc, CD 1.

LESSON 6

1. Hugo, *Les Misérables: A New Unabridged Translation*, 110.
2. Ibid.
3. Ibid.
4. C. S. Lewis, *Yours, Jack* (New York: HarperCollins, 2009), 309.
5. Hugo, *Les Misérables: A New Unabridged Translation*, 113.
6. Ibid.

LESSON 7

1. Hugo, *Les Misérables: A New Unabridged Translation*, 13.
2. "Prologue–Work Song," *Les Misérables: The Original 1985 London Cast Recording*, 2012, compact disc.
3. Hugo, *Les Misérables: A New Unabridged Translation*, 75, 104.
4. Ibid., 105.
5. Ibid., 226.
6. Ibid., 79.
7. Ibid., 80.

LESSON 8

1. Hugo, *Les Misérables: A New Unabridged Translation*, 52.
2. Ibid., 103.
3. Ibid., 103, 104.
4. Ibid., 104.
5. Ibid., 52.

LESSON 9

1. Hugo, *Les Misérables: A New Unabridged Translation*, 225.
2. Ibid., 165.
3. Victor Hugo, *Les Misérables: The Classic Story of the Triumph of Grace and Redemption: Adapted for Today's Readers*, ed. Jim Reimann (Nashville: Thomas Nelson, 2001).

4. Hugo, *Les Misérables: A New Unabridged Translation*, 1004.

5. Ibid., 222.

6. Ibid., 226, 227.

7. Victor Hugo, *Les Misérables: A Novel: Complete in One Volume*, trans. Charles H. Wilbour (New York: Carleton, 1863), 159.

8. Hugo, *Les Misérables: A New Unabridged Translation*, 227.

9. "Tax Cheating Statistics," Statistic Brain, researched April 19, 2013, http://www.statisticbrain.com/how-many-people-cheat-on-taxes/.

10. "Josephson Institute of Ethics Releases Study on High School Character and Adult Conduct: Character Study Reveals Predictors of Lying and Cheating," The Josephson Institute, October 29, 2009, http://josephsoninstitute.org/surveys/.

11. Gary Belsky, "Why (Almost) All of Us Cheat and Steal: Behavioral Economist Dan Ariely Talks About Why Everyone's Willing to Cheat a Little, Why You'll Steal a Staple from Work but Not Petty Cash and Whether Punishments for Cheating Actually Work," *Time* Business & Money, June 18, 2012, http://business.time.com/2012/06/18/why-almost-all-of-us-cheat-and-steal/.

Lesson 10

1. "Valjean's Soliloquy (What Have I Done?)" *Les Misérables* (musical), music by Claude-Michel Schönberg, English lyrics by Herbert Kretzmer, French lyrics by Alain Boublil, 1980.

2. Hugo, *Les Misérables: A New Unabridged Translation*, 164.

3. "Valjean Arrested, Valjean Forgiven," *Les Misérables* (musical), music by Claude-Michel Schönberg, English lyrics by Herbert Kretzmer, French lyrics by Alain Boublil, 1980.

4. Bob Welch, "Chance at Eugene Mission 'a Miracle': The New Executive Director Shares How His and His Wife's Spiritual Conversion Led Them Here," *Register-Guard,* Eugene, Oregon, April 24, 2011, A1.

5. Ibid.

6. Oswald Chambers, "The Initiative Against Dreaming," *My Utmost for His Highest* website, February 20, 2013, http://.org /classic/the-initiative-against-dreaming-classic/.

Lesson 11

1. Hugo, *Les Misérables: A New Unabridged Translation*, 165.
2. Ibid.

Lesson 12

1. Victor Hugo, *Les Misérables*, excerpted from Mukherjee, *Longman Supplementary Reader 5* (India: Pearson Education, 2006), 47.
2. Hugo, *Les Misérables: A New Unabridged Translation*, 122.
3. Ibid.
4. Ibid., 143.
5. Ibid., 143, 144.
6. "I Dreamed a Dream," *Les Misérables* (musical), music by Claude-Michel Schönberg, English lyrics by Herbert Kretzmer, French lyrics by Alain Boublil, 1980.
7. Hugo, *Les Misérables: A New Unabridged Translation*, 149.
8. "Reading Guide: *Les Misérables*," Penguin Group, http://www .us.penguingroup.com/static/rguides/us/les_miserables.html.
9. Hugo, *Les Misérables: A New Unabridged Translation*, 477.

Lesson 13

1. Hugo, *Les Misérables: A New Unabridged Translation*, 178.
2. Ibid.
3. *Les Misérables*, directed by Tom Hooper (Hollywood: Universal Pictures, 2012), DVD.
4. Hugo, *Les Misérables: A New Unabridged Translation*, 194.
5. Ibid., 197.
6. Ibid., 198.
7. Ibid.
8. Ibid., 199.
9. Oswald Chambers, "The Uncritical Temper," *My Utmost for His*

Highest website, June 17, 2013, http://utmost.org/classic/the
-uncritical-temper-classic/.

10. Philip Yancey, *What's So Amazing About Grace?* (Grand Rapids:
Zondervan, 2008).

11. Henri J. M. Nouwen, *The Return of the Prodigal Son: A Story of
Homecoming*, reissue ed. (New York: Image Books/Doubleday,
1994), 105.

Lesson 14

1. Hugo, *Les Misérables: A New Unabridged Translation*, 189.

Lesson 15

1. Hugo, *Les Misérables: A New Unabridged Translation*, 202.

2. Ibid., 190.

3. "I Dreamed a Dream," *Les Misérables* (musical), music by Claude-
Michel Schönberg, English lyrics by Herbert Kretzmer, French
lyrics by Alain Boublil, 1980.

4. Hugo, *Les Misérables: A New Unabridged Translation*, 190.

5. Anne Lamott, *Traveling Mercies: Some Thoughts on Faith* (New
York: Anchor Books, 2000).

6. Philip Yancey, *What's So Amazing About Grace?* (Grand Rapids:
Zondervan, 2008).

7. David A. Seamands and Beth Funk, *Healing for Damaged
Emotions Workbook* (Colorado Springs: David C. Cook, 1992), 43.

8. Philip Yancey, *What's So Amazing About Grace?* (Grand Rapids:
Zondervan, 2008).

Lesson 16

1. Hugo, *Les Misérables: A New Unabridged Translation*, 171.

2. Ibid., 292, 293.

3. Ibid., 634.

Lesson 17

1. Hugo, *Les Misérables: A New Unabridged Translation*, 358.

2. Ibid., 356.

3. Ibid., 357.

4. Ibid., 358.

5. Paul L. Wachtel, *The Poverty of Affluence: A Psychological Portrait of the American Way of Life* (British Columbia: New Society, 1989).

LESSON 18

1. Hugo, *Les Misérables: A New Unabridged Translation*, 373.

2. Ibid., 372.

3. Ibid., 373.

4. Ibid.

5. Ibid.

LESSON 19

1. Hugo, *Les Misérables: A New Unabridged Translation*, 379.

2. Ibid., 378.

3. Ibid., 380.

4. Ibid., 381–82.

5. Ibid., 382.

6. Ibid., 379, 381.

7. Paul L. Wachtel, *The Poverty of Affluence: A Psychological Portrait of the American Way of Life* (British Columbia: New Society, 1989).

8. Ibid.

LESSON 20

1. Hugo, *Les Misérables: A New Unabridged Translation*, 390.

2. Ibid., 383.

3. Ibid., 386.

4. Ibid., 390.

5. Ibid.

6. Ibid.

7. Ibid., 395.

8. Ibid., 396–97.

9. Ibid., 421.

LESSON 21

1. Victor Hugo, *Les Misérables: A Novel: Complete in One Volume*, trans. Charles H. Wilbour (New York: Carleton, 1863), 67.
2. Hugo, *Les Misérables: A New Unabridged Translation*, 405.
3. Ibid., 409.
4. Rachael Rettner, "Are Today's Youth Less Creative & Imaginative?" *Live Science*, August 12, 2011, http://www .livescience.com/15535-children-creative.html.

LESSON 22

1. Hugo, *Les Misérables: A New Unabridged Translation*, 437.
2. "Valjean's Soliloquy (What Have I Done?)" music by Claude-Michel Schönberg, English lyrics by Herbert Kretzmer, French lyrics by Alain Boublil, 1980.
3. Hugo, *Les Misérables: A New Unabridged Translation*, 436.
4. Ibid.
5. Ibid., 437.
6. Ibid., 436.
7. Ibid., 439.

LESSON 23

1. Hugo, *Les Misérables: A New Unabridged Translation*, 519.
2. Addison H. Hart, "Sentiments Abstractly Christian: Victor Hugo, Les Misérables, and the Catholic Imagination," *Touchstone* archives, accessed November 3, 2013, http://www.touchstonemag .com/archives/article.php?id=11-03-018-f.
3. G. K. Chesterton, "The Ways of the World: Victor Hugo," *Nash's Pall Mall Magazine*, January–April 1902, 563.
4. Thomas Merton, *Opening the Bible* (Collegeville, MN: Liturgical Press, 1986), 52.
5. Hugo, *Les Misérables: A New Unabridged Translation*, 521.
6. Ibid.
7. Ibid., 519.
8. Ibid., 487.
9. Ibid., 511.

10. Ibid., 522.
11. Oswald Chambers, "The Consecration of Spiritual Energy," *My Utmost for His Highest* website, November 27, 2012, http://utmost .org/classic/the-consecration-of-spiritual-energy-classic/.

LESSON 24

1. All quotes in this lesson are from the following article: Bob Welch, "What Would Sister Aileen Do?" *Register-Guard*, Eugene, Oregon, June 30, 2013, http://www.registerguard.com/rg/news /local/30095925-152/sister-aileen-welch-beymer-peacehealth .html.csp; no longer accessible.

LESSON 25

1. Hugo, *Les Misérables: A New Unabridged Translation*, 468.
2. Ibid., 467.
3. Ibid., 465.
4. Ibid., 468.

LESSON 26

1. Hugo, *Les Misérables: A New Unabridged Translation*, 547.
2. Ibid.
3. Ibid., 168.
4. "Valjean Arrested, Valjean Forgiven," *Les Misérables* (musical), music by Claude-Michel Schönberg, English lyrics by Herbert Kretzmer, French lyrics by Alain Boublil, 1980.
5. Annie Dillard, *The Writing Life* (New York: Harper Perennial, 2013).

LESSON 27

1. Hugo, *Les Misérables: A New Unabridged Translation*, 525.
2. Ibid.

LESSON 28

1. Hugo, *Les Misérables: A New Unabridged Translation*, 573.
2. Ibid., 567.
3. Ibid., 572.

4. Ibid., 573.

5. Ann Voskamp, "About Ann," *One Thousand Gifts* website, accessed November 3, 2013, http://onethousandgifts.com/about.

6. Ann Voskamp, *One Thousand Gifts Devotional: Reflections on Finding Everyday Graces* (Grand Rapids: Zondervan, 2012).

Lesson 29

1. Hugo, *Les Misérables: A New Unabridged Translation*, 569.

2. Ibid.

3. Ibid., 570.

4. Ibid., 569.

5. Ibid., 571.

6. Ibid., 571, 573.

7. Ibid., 573.

8. Aleksandr Solzhenitsyn, *The Gulag Archipelago 1918–1956: An Experiment in Literary Investigation*, vol. 1 (New York: Basic Books, 1997), 168.

9. Aleksandr Solzhenitsyn, trans. A. Klimoff, "'Men Have Forgotten God'—The Templeon Address," *Orthodox America*, accessed November 3, 2013, http://www.roca.org/OA/36/36h.htm.

Lesson 30

1. Hugo, *Les Misérables: A New Unabridged Translation*, 678.

2. Oswald Chambers, "Getting into God's Stride," *My Utmost for His Highest* website, October 12, 2013, http://utmost.org/classic/getting-into-god%E2%80%99s-stride-classic/.

3. Hugo, *Les Misérables: A New Unabridged Translation*, 372.

4. Ibid., 51.

5. Oswald Chambers, "The Place of Exaltation," *My Utmost for His Highest* website, October 1, 2013, http://utmost.org/the-place-of-exaltation/.

6. Oswald Chambers, "The Way of Abraham," *My Utmost for His Highest* website, March 19, 2013, http://utmost.org/classic/the-way-of-abraham-in-faith-classic/.

7. Bob Welch, *Where Roots Grow Deep: Stories of Family, Love, and Legacy* (Eugene, OR: Harvest House Publishers, 1999).

LESSON 31

1. Hugo, *Les Misérables: A New Unabridged Translation*, 594.
2. Ibid.
3. Ibid.
4. Ibid.
5. Ibid., 594, 680.
6. Graham Robb, *Victor Hugo: A Biography* (New York: W. W. Norton, 1999), 382.
7. Hugo, *Les Misérables: A New Unabridged Translation*, 593.

LESSON 32

1. Hugo, *Les Misérables: A New Unabridged Translation*, 615.
2. Ibid., 614.
3. Ibid., 615.
4. Ibid.
5. Bob Welch, *Easy Company Soldier: The Legendary Battles of a Sergeant from WWII's "Band of Brothers"* (New York: St. Martin's Griffin, 2008).

LESSON 33

1. Hugo, *Les Misérables: A New Unabridged Translation*, 615.
2. Ibid., 611.
3. Ibid., 615.
4. Ibid., 616, 617.

LESSON 34

1. Hugo, *Les Misérables: A New Unabridged Translation*, 629.
2. Ibid., 627.
3. Ibid.
4. Ibid., 629.
5. Ibid., 630, 634.
6. Ibid., 631.

LESSON 35

1. Hugo, *Les Misérables: A New Unabridged Translation*, 629.

2. Ibid.

3. C. S. Lewis, *The Business of Heaven: Daily Readings from C. S. Lewis* (Orlando: Houghton Mifflin Harcourt, 1984), 209.

4. Jim Wallis, *The Soul of Politics: Beyond "Religious Right" and "Secular Left"* (Boston: Mariner, 1995).

5. Hugo, *Les Misérables: A New Unabridged Translation*, 629.

LESSON 36

1. "Bring Him Home," *Les Misérables* (musical), music by Claude-Michel Schönberg, English lyrics by Herbert Kretzmer, French lyrics by Alain Boublil, 1980.

2. Susanne Alleyn, "No, It's Not Actually the French Revolution: *Les Misérables* and History," *Blague* (blog), January 3, 2013, http://www.susannealleyn.com/blog.htm?post=891473.

3. Ibid.

4. Hugo, *Les Misérables: A New Unabridged Translation*, xvii.

5. Martin Luther King Jr., "I Have a Dream," speech delivered on August 28, 1963.

6. Dave Burchett, *When Bad Christians Happen to Good People: Where We Have Failed Each Other and How to Reverse the Damage* (New York: Random House, 2002), 222–23.

7. Henri J. M. Nouwen, in Joel L. Huffstetler, *Boundless Love: The Parable of the Prodigal Son and Reconciliation* (Lanham, MD: University Press of America, 2008), 42.

8. Brennan Manning, *Abba's Child: The Cry of the Heart for Intimate Belonging*, exp. ed. (Colorado Springs: NavPress, 2009).

9. Hugo, *Les Misérables: A New Unabridged Translation*, 675.

10. Oswald Chambers, "Divine Reasonings of Faith," *My Utmost for His Highest* website, May 21, 2013, http://utmost.org/classic/divine-reasonings-of-faith-classic/.

11. Oswald Chambers, "Isn't There Some Misunderstanding?" *My Utmost for His Highest* website, March 28, 2013, http://utmost.org/classic/isn%E2%80%99t-there-some-misunderstanding-classic/.

Lesson 37

1. Victor Hugo, *Les Misérables: Classic Book*, episode 3, bk. 8, chap. 1, on SparkNotes, http://pd.sparknotes.com/lit/lesmis/section24.html.
2. Victor Hugo, *Les Misérables: A Novel: Complete in One Volume*, trans. Charles H. Wilbour (New York: Carleton, 1863), 744.
3. "*Les Miserables: Novel Summary: Section 3 - Book Eight*," Novel Guide, http://www.novelguide.com/les-miserables/summaries /section3-bookeight.
4. Hugo, *Les Misérables: A New Unabridged Translation*, 759; Hugo, *Les Misérables: A Novel: Complete in One Volume*, trans. Charles H. Wilbour (New York: Carleton, 1863), 115.
5. Hugo, *Les Misérables: A New Unabridged Translation*, 769.

Lesson 38

1. Hugo, *Les Misérables: A New Unabridged Translation*, 219.
2. Ibid., 595.
3. Hugo, *Les Misérables: The Only Complete and Unabridged Paperback Edition* (New York: Signet, 1987), 920.
4. Hugo, *Les Misérables: A New Unabridged Translation*, 595.
5. Ibid.
6. George Klin and Amy Louise Marsland, *CliffsNotes on Hugo's* Les Miserables (Boston: Houghton Mifflin Harcourt, 2007), 48.
7. Victor Hugo, *Les Misérables: The Only Complete and Unabridged Paperback Edition* (New York: Signet, 1987), 947.

Lesson 39

1. Hugo, *Les Misérables: A New Unabridged Translation*, 894.
2. Ibid., 899.
3. Ibid.
4. C. S. Lewis, *The Four Loves*, 2nd printing ed. (Boston: Mariner, 1971), 121.
5. Hugo, *Les Misérables: A New Unabridged Translation*, 939.

Lesson 40

1. Hugo, *Les Misérables: A New Unabridged Translation*, 904.
2. Ibid., 901.

3. Ibid.

4. Ibid.

5. Oswald Chambers, "The Habit of Wealth," *My Utmost for His Highest* website, May 16, 2013, http://utmost.org/classic/the-habit-of-wealth-classic/.

6. Oswald Chambers, *The Quotable Oswald Chambers*, comp. and ed. David McCasland, Har/Cdr ed. (Grand Rapids: Discovery House, 2008).

7. "I Dreamed a Dream," *Les Misérables* (musical), music by Claude-Michel Schönberg, English lyrics by Herbert Kretzmer, French lyrics by Alain Boublil, 1980.

8. Oswald Chambers, *The Quotable Oswald Chambers*, comp. and ed. David McCasland, Har/Cdr ed. (Grand Rapids: Discovery House, 2008).

LESSON 41

1. Victor Hugo, *Les Misérables: Authorized Translation* (New York: Albert Cogswell, 1879), 676.

2. Hugo, *Les Misérables: A New Unabridged Translation*, 1031.

3. Ibid., 1032.

4. Ibid.

5. Hugo, *Les Misérables: A Novel: Complete in One Volume*, trans. Charles H. Wilbour (New York: Carleton, 1863), 118.

6. Ibid., 119.

7. Ibid.

8. Ibid., 120.

9. Hugo, *Les Misérables: A New Unabridged Translation*, 1038.

LESSON 42

1. Hugo, *Les Misérables: A New Unabridged Translation*, 1031.

2. Walter Scott, *Marmion*, canto 6, stanza 17 (1830).

3. Hugo, *Les Misérables: A New Unabridged Translation*, 683.

LESSON 43

1. Hugo, *Les Misérables: A New Unabridged Translation*, 875.

2. Ibid., 156.

3. Ibid.

4. See, for example, Terra Johnson, "Love and Tragedy: Marius x Eponine," *Ship Manifesto* (blog), August, 13, 2005, http://ship-manifesto.livejournal.com/107276.html.

5. "In My Life"/"A Heart Full of Love," *Les Misérables* (musical), act 1, English lyrics by Herbert Kretzmer.

6. "The Confrontation," English lyrics by Herbert Kretzmer, *Les Misérables Live! Dream the Dream* (2010 Cast Album, New 25th Anniversary Production), compact disc, CD 1.

Lesson 44

1. Victor Marie Hugo, *Les Misérables [tr. by C. E. Wilbour]: Fantine; Cosette & Marius. Jean Valjean; Cosette and Marius* (London: Ward, Lock, & Tyler, 1876), 326.

2. Ibid., 260.

3. "Bring Him Home," *Les Misérables* (musical), act 2, English lyrics by Herbert Kretzmer.

4. Anna Tims, "How We Made *Les Misérables*," *Guardian* (UK), Stage, February 18, 2013, http://www.theguardian.com/stage/2013/feb/18/how-we-made-les-miserables.

5. The story and quotes that follow are from Bob Welch, "Actor Brings North a Bit of Broadway," *Register-Guard*, Eugene, Oregon, February 2003, available at Free Library, http://www.thefreelibrary.com/Actor+brings+North+a+bit+of+Broadway.-a098300239.

6. Victor Marie Hugo, *Les Misérables [tr. by C. E. Wilbour]: Fantine; Cosette & Marius. Jean Valjean; Cosette and Marius* (London: Ward, Lock, & Tyler, 1876), 531.

7. Remaining quotes in this lesson are from Welch, "Actor Brings North a Bit of Broadway."

Lesson 45

1. Hugo, *Les Misérables: A New Unabridged Translation*, 1291.

2. Ibid., 1302.

3. Ibid., 1257, 1297.

4. Oswald Chambers, "All Noble Things Are Difficult," *My Utmost for His Highest* website, July 7, 2013, http://utmost.org/classic/all -noble-things-are-difficult-classic/.

5. Donna Newman, "'Les Mis' Begins Six-Week Run at Theatre Three," *Times Beacon-Record*, September 18, 2013, http://www .northshoreoflongisland.com/Articles-Arts-and-Lifestyles-i-2013-09-19 -97212.112114-sub-Les-Mis-begins-sixweek-run-at-Theatre-Three.html.

Lesson 46

1. Hugo, *Les Misérables: A New Unabridged Translation*, 569.

2. Oswald Chambers, "The Ministry of the Unnoticed," *My Utmost for His Highest* website, August 21, 2013, http://utmost.org/the -ministry-of-the-unnoticed/.

Lesson 47

1. Hugo, *Les Misérables: A New Unabridged Translation*, 55.

2. Oswald Chambers, "The Mystery of Believing" (sermon), sermonindex.net, accessed November 5, 2013, http://www .sermonindex.net/modules/newbb/viewtopic.php?topic_id =34437&forum=45&0.

Lesson 48

1. Hugo, *Les Misérables: A New Unabridged Translation*, 1232.

2. Victor Marie Hugo, *Les Misérables [tr. by C. E. Wilbour]: Fantine; Cosette & Marius. Jean Valjean; Cosette and Marius* (London: Ward, Lock, & Tyler, 1876), 315.

3. *"Les Miserables* Film Tie-in: Reading Notes: Book Club Notes for *Les Misérables* by Victor Hugo Book Summary" (United Kingdom: Penguin Books Australia, 2012), http://www.penguin .com.au/products/9780141392608/les-miserables-film-tie/340208 /reading-notes, accessed November 5, 2013.

4. "The Bishop," *Les Misérables* (musical), music by Claude-Michel Schönberg, English lyrics by Herbert Kretzmer, French lyrics by Alain Boublil, 1980.

5. "Lead on, O King Eternal," lyrics by Ernest W. Shurtleff (1862–1917), music by Henry T. Smart (1813–1879).

6. Henri J. M. Nouwen, *In the Name of Jesus* (London: Darton, Longman and Todd, 1989).

7. Cal Thomas and Ed Dobson, *Blinded by Might: Why the Religious Right Can't Save America*, 2nd ed. (Grand Rapids: Zondervan, 2000), 84.

LESSON 49

1. Hugo, *Les Misérables: A New Unabridged Translation*, 167.

2. "Suddenly," music by Claude-Michel Schönberg, lyrics by Herbert Kretzmer and Alain Boublil, from *Les Misérables*, directed by Tom Hooper (Hollywood: Universal Pictures, 2012), DVD.

3. "Valjean's Soliloquy," music by Claude-Michel Schönberg, lyrics by Herbert Kretzmer and Alain Boublil, 1980.

4. Ibid. "Javert's Suicide."

5. Aleksandr Solzhenitsyn, in Chris Abbott, *21 Speeches That Shaped Our World: The People and Ideas That Changed the Way We Think* (New York: Random House, 2010), 88.

6. "Javert's Suicide," *Les Misérables* (musical), music by Claude-Michel Schönberg, lyrics by Herbert Kretzmer and Alain Boublil, 1980.

7. Don E. Eberly, *Restoring the Good Society: A New Vision for Politics and Culture* (Ada, MI: Baker, 1994).

8. Cal Thomas and Ed Dobson, *Blinded by Might: Why the Religious Right Can't Save America*, 2nd ed. (Grand Rapids: Zondervan, 2000), 122.

LESSON 50

1. Hugo, *Les Misérables*, as quoted in "Book Bites: *Les Miserables*," *Shesourceful* (blog), December 26, 2012, http://shesourceful.com /2012/12/26/book-bites-les-miserables/.

2. Hugo, *Les Misérables: A New Unabridged Translation*, 1452.

LESSON 51

1. Hugo, *Les Misérables: A New Unabridged Translation*, 1170.
2. "Valjean's Death," *Les Misérables Wiki*, http://lesmiserables.wikia .com/wiki/Valjean's_Death.
3. "Epilogue" (Finale) from *Les Misérables*, directed by Tom Hooper (Hollywood: Universal Pictures, 2012), DVD.
4. Victor Hugo, *Les Misérables: A Novel: Complete in One Volume*, trans. Charles H. Wilbour (New York: Carleton, 1863), 7.
5. "ABC Café/Red and Black," *Les Misérables Wiki*, http://lesmiserables .wikia.com/wiki/ABC_Caf%C3%A9_/_Red_and_Black.
6. Henri J. M. Nouwen, *The Return of the Prodigal Son: A Story of Homecoming*, reissue ed. (New York: Image Books/Doubleday, 1994), 42.
7. David Helm, "The Gospel in Seven Words," *Christian Century*, August 23, 2012, http://www.christiancentury.org/article/2012 -08/gospel-seven-words.

LESSON 52

1. Hugo, *Les Misérables*, bk. 9, chap. 5, p. 1458, as quoted on "Quotes from *Les Miserables*," http://www.oocities.org/westhollywood /park/4363/lesmis.html.
2. Hugo, *Les Misérables: A New Unabridged Translation*, 1427; *Les Misérables: A Novel: Complete in One Volume*, trans. Charles H. Wilbour (New York: Carleton, 1863), 147.
3. Hugo, *Les Misérables: A New Unabridged Translation*, 1427.
4. Ibid., 1432.
5. Ibid., 1462.
6. Hugo, *Les Misérables: The Only Complete and Unabridged Paperback Edition* (New York: Signet, 1987), 1, 460.
7. Hugo, *Les Misérables: A New Unabridged Translation*, 573.
8. Victor Marie Hugo, *Les Misérables [tr. by C. E. Wilbour]: Fantine; Cosette & Marius. Jean Valjean; Cosette and Marius* (London: Ward, Lock, & Tyler, 1876), 535.
9. Ibid., 536.

10. Hugo, *Les Misérables*, bk. 9, chap. 5, p. 1458.
11. "Valjean's Death," *Les Misérables Wiki*, http://lesmiserables.wikia
    .com/wiki/Valjean's_Death.
12. Hugo, *Les Misérables: A New Unabridged Translation*, 74.

Book Club Questions

 1. Hugo, *Les Misérables: A New Unabridged Translation*, 52.